Training in America

Anthony P. Carnevale
Leila J. Gainer
Janice Villet

Training in America

The Organization and Strategic Role of Training

 Jossey-Bass Publishers

San Francisco • Oxford • 1990

TRAINING IN AMERICA
The Organization and Strategic Role of Training
by Anthony P. Carnevale, Leila J. Gainer, and Janice Villet

Copyright © 1990 by: Jossey-Bass Inc., Publishers
                350 Sansome Street
                San Francisco, California 94104

                Jossey-Bass Limited
                Headington Hill Hall
                Oxford OX3 0BW

                American Society for Training and Development
                1630 Duke Street
                Box 1443
                Alexandria, Virginia 22313

Library of Congress Cataloging-in-Publication Data

Carnevale, Anthony Patrick.
    Training in America : the organization and strategic role of
training / Anthony P. Carnevale, Leila J. Gainer, Janice Villet. —
1st ed.
        p.   cm. — (The Jossey-Bass management series)
    Includes bibliographical references.
    ISBN 1-55542-203-9 (alk. paper)
    1. Employees—Training of—United States.   2. Occupational
training—United States.   I. Gainer, Leila J.   II. Villet, Janice.
III. Title.   IV. Series.
HF5549.5.T7C2984   1990
658.3'124—dc20   89-28662
                                             CIP

Manufactured in the United States of America

JACKET DESIGN BY WILLI BAUM

FIRST EDITION

Code 9011

The Jossey-Bass Management Series

ASTD Best Practices Series:
Training for a Changing Work Force

The material in this project was prepared under Grant No. 99-6-0705-75-079-02 from the Employment and Training Administration, U.S. Department of Labor, under the authority of Title IV, part D, of the Job Training Partnership Act of 1982. Grantees undertaking such projects under government sponsorship are encouraged to express freely their professional judgment. Therefore, points of view or opinions stated in this document do not necessarily represent the official position or policy of the Department of Labor.

Contents

Preface

Employers spend $30 billion on formal training and approximately $180 billion on informal on-the-job training each year. Research has already shown that learning in school and on the job is by far the most important factor accounting for American economic growth and productivity in this century. Specialists in the training field also accept research that shows that human resource efforts account for two-thirds of the nation's productivity improvements since 1929 and that workers must be highly skilled for productivity to remain high. But in spite of all this, little has been done to catalogue who gets training and how much, let alone what employer training systems look like. Until now, no overview of training and its strategic role has ever been compiled and published.

The primary purpose of *Training in America: The Organization and Strategic Role of Training* is to provide an overview of training in America, in terms of both who gets trained and how the training itself is organized, structured, and delivered. Discussions are bolstered with facts and figures that give rise to the economic implications training has for industry and the American economy as a whole. Second, this book explores how training can be used to achieve the strategic goals of an organization. Third, it examines why and how companies use outside resources to provide training to their employees. Practical examples and case studies are used to illustrate the characteristics of these learning situations and to capture the essence of the training industry's contributions to employer institutions. Finally, this book sets forth a comprehensive training and development policy that expands and integrates the roles of government, industry, and educational institutions.

This book is the result of research underwritten by a grant from the U.S. Department of Labor (DOL) and conducted under the auspices of the American Society for Training and Development (ASTD), a nonprofit professional association representing approximately fifty thousand practitioners, managers, administrators, educators, and researchers in the field of human resource development.

The information in this volume reflects only some of the findings gathered during a thirty-month research effort that explored training practices in America's employer institutions. Other findings are detailed in volumes on technical training, basic workplace skills, and a workplace basics manual, which together provide a step-by-step process for establishing a basic skills training program in the workplace. Other findings are detailed in two companion books, *Workplace Basics: The Essential Skills Employers Want* and *Training the Technical Work Force*, and a companion manual, *Workplace Basics Training Manual*, that provides a step-by-step process for establishing a basic skills training program in the work place (all published by Jossey-Bass). In addition, findings are detailed in five booklets published in 1988 and 1989: *Workplace Basics: The Skills Employers Want, The Learning Enterprise, Training America, Training Partnerships: Linking Employers and Providers,* and *The Next Economy* (all available from ASTD, 1630 Duke Street, Box 1443, Alexandria, Va. 22313).

How Our Research Was Conducted

The ASTD-DOL research project was staffed by a team of ten professionals and support staff. This team was greatly assisted by ASTD members who volunteered their expertise and provided access to their corporations. In addition, experts from the fields of economics, adult education, training, public policy, and strategic management contributed analyses that provided a contextual backdrop for our work.

In 1986 when we launched this project, we did so with a determination that we would conduct applied research. Throughout the project, we kept our sights firmly focused on the real world. We began by surveying the current literature, looking for trends and patterns; this effort helped us to identify the leaders in various disciplines and draw some preliminary conclusions. We tested our preliminary findings by asking a cadre of experts drawn from ASTD's membership to identify other experts and practitioners who might provide feedback and insights. We continued along this path, and our list of contacts grew. From these we formed advisory panels that met during 1987 to advise us on our direction and findings. We also built networks of more than four hundred experts and practitioners — the organization and strategic role area network alone had seventy-eight members — who were mailed periodic updates of findings and asked for feedback.

Corporations and other private and public employer institutions were tapped extensively to provide actual examples of successful training systems and practices. We conducted some on-site studies and many telephone interviews, using specially constructed interview instruments that ensured we would gather uniform information. These employer "snapshots" are used throughout the book to complement and illustrate our findings and support the theoretical underpinnings of our work. We enlisted over thirty experts and practitioners to review and comment as we developed our first draft reports. Their insights also are reflected in this book.

Who Should Read This Book

The findings in *Training in America: The Organization and Strategic Role of Training* are designed to provide readers with an understanding of the size and scope of training in America, who the trainees are and how much is invested in their training, and how training supports the strategic directions pursued by employers. It is a reference work with facts and figures as well as a guide for forging relationships with training providers and understanding the strategic decision-making process. Its intended audience includes executives and managers in all kinds of public and private organizations; human resource development training practitioners; personnel and human resource management practitioners; organization development practitioners; business and management consultants; college and university administrators; academics in the fields of education, business management, industrial relations, public administration, and other areas; and educational leaders and policymakers.

Organization and Content

This book should be viewed as a compendium of facts, figures, and suggestions. By its very nature, it explores disparate subjects; therefore, it is organized into parts to provide a clear delineation between the subject groupings.

Part One provides an overview of the key players in training. It comprises three chapters. Chapter One explores institutions that provide training that qualifies people to enter the work force and upgrades or updates employee skills. In Chapter Two we look at the history of employer-based training and how it is structured (for example, centralized or decentralized) inside employer institutions. The chapter also provides a discussion of the applied approach to learning, which is central to workplace training. Chapter Three examines the various categories of workers (for example, executives, professionals, clericals, craft workers, and so on) who receive training, the types of training they receive, and how much employers spend for each trainee category.

The three chapters in Part Two provide a look at the relationships between employers and training providers. In Chapter Four we explore how training providers and employers develop partnerships and "learning linkages" to deliver job-specific training. Chapter Five describes the different providers used by employers for upgrading training and contains snapshots of actual linkages between employers and providers. In Chapter Six we discuss the distinguishing characteristics of linkages, for example, how employers select providers based on the type of training needed.

In Part Three we provide some of the background and techniques needed to become a strategic player. Chapter Seven is a primer on the competitive strategies that employers utilize. It examines training as a tool for achieving strategic goals.

Chapter Eight helps trainers answer important questions before attempting to influence the strategic decision-making process. Chapter Nine explores practical approaches to connecting training to the strategic decision-making process.

Composed of one chapter, Part Four suggests ways in which business, education, and government can improve training. In Chapter Ten we provide policy recommendations to support the learning demands of our changing society.

Acknowledgments

Special thanks to Shari L. Holland, who served as research assistant on the project; Dawn Temple, Kimberly Genevro, and Stacey Wagner, who provided administrative assistance; Diane L. Charles, who reviewed portions of the publication and managed our research symposium as well as the production aspects of report preparation; Eileen West and Richard West of West Training and Logistics Systems, who assisted with corporate examples; Diane Kirrane, who provided editorial assistance; and Gerald Gundersen and Raymond Uhalde of the U.S. Department of Labor, who provided insights and guidance along the way.

The project team also wishes to acknowledge the contributions of the following experts, who consulted with us and provided contextual analyses for the organization and strategic role area of study: Harold Goldstein, former assistant commissioner of the U.S. Bureau of Labor Statistics; Robert Craig, former vice-president (retired) of the American Society for Training and Development; Debra Cohen, Carolyn Erdener, and John A. Pearce of George Mason University School of Business Administration; Thomas J. Cosse of the E. Caliborne Robins School of Business, University of Richmond; Janet Johnston of the National Commission for Employment Policy; and Patrice Flynn of the University of Texas, Austin.

Finally, we want to thank our advisory panel and network participants, who contributed their advice and counsel.

Alexandria, Virginia   Anthony P. Carnevale
January 1990   Leila J. Gainer
                        Janice Villet

The Authors

Anthony P. Carnevale was project director and principal investigator for the ASTD-DOL project. Carnevale is chief economist and vice-president of national affairs for ASTD. He also currently serves as a board member of the National Center on Education and Employment at Columbia University; the National Center on Education and the Economy, co-chaired by Mario Cuomo and John Scully; and the National Commission on the Skills of the American Work Force, comprised of America's leading business executives, union leaders, and education and government officials.

Prior to joining ASTD, Carnevale was the government affairs director for the American Federation of State, County, and Municipal Employees (AFSCME). He also served as a comoderator for the White House Conference on Productivity and the chairman of the Fiscal Policy Task Force for the U.S. Council on Competitiveness. Carnevale has held positions as the senior policy analyst at the U.S. Department of Health, Education, and Welfare; the senior staff economist for the U.S. House of Representatives' Government Operations Committee; and the senior staff member for education, employment, training, and social services for the U.S. Senate Committee on the Budget. He also served as a high school teacher and social worker in his home state of Maine. Carnevale was coauthor of the principal affidavit in *Rodriguez* v. *San Antonio,* a U.S. Supreme Court action to remedy unequal tax burdens and education benefits.

Carnevale has a Ph.D. degree, with a concentration in public finance economics, from the Maxwell School of Public

Affairs, Syracuse University. He holds an M.A. degree in social science and an M.A. degree in public administration from Syracuse University and a B.A. degree in intellectual and cultural history from Colby College.

Leila J. Gainer managed the daily operations of the ASTD-DOL project. Gainer is ASTD's director of national affairs. She serves as a member of the advisory board for the Center for Business and Government Services of the Northern Virginia Community College and as a member of the National Alliance of Business advisory committee on structural work-based learning. In 1989, she also served as an informal advisor to ABC and PBS for the Project Literacy U.S. (PLUS) Campaign.

Before joining ASTD, Gainer directed the Center for Regional Action for the National Association of Regional Councils (NARC), working with elected officials at the state and local government levels around the nation. In her nine years at NARC, Gainer served as director of federal liaison, communications, and research; Washington information coordinator; and editor of the *Washington Report*. While at NARC, Gainer was honored by President Carter for her efforts leading to passage of the Rural Development Act of 1980. Gainer served as a reporter and editor for Commerce Clearing House's (CCH) biweekly publications *College and University Report* and *Commodity Futures*. In the early 1970s, she was managing editor of CCH's *Labor Law Guide* and on the staff of *Labor Law Report*. Gainer has a B.A. degree from Frostburg State College, Maryland.

Janice Villet edited the manuscript for this book. She is a writer, researcher, and editor for ASTD. Prior to joining the ASTD-DOL project, Villet was special projects coordinator for the National Association of Regional Councils, where she authored *Making the Link: Coordinating Economic Development and Employment and Training* and *Data on Regional Councils*. Villet also was a legislative analyst for NARC and editor of the annual white paper on regional council issues. She served as manager for that association's annual federal briefing, which focused on the fiscal crisis and the budget deficit. Before joining NARC, Villet was a staff member of the U.S. Senate Committee on Commerce, Science, and Transportation. She also held the position of researcher for the National Association of Counties, where she authored *The Recreation Game: A Guide for Local Governments,* and was staff liaison for that association's county recreation and park officials. Villet served as legislative aide for the National Recreation and Park Association. Villet has a B.S. degree from the University of Missouri, Columbia.

Organization and Strategic Role Advisory Panel

Jack Bowsher
Director of Education
International Business Machines
 Corporation

Donald Conover
Vice-President
Education and Training
American Telephone & Telegraph

Gerald Gundersen
Chief, Research
U.S. Department of Labor

Gerald Hinch
Assistant Director
Office of Training and Development
U.S. Office of Personnel Management

John Hurley
Director
Corporate Training and Educational
 Resources
Chase Manhattan Corporation

Mathew Juechter
Managing Director
Integration Resource Associates

Kenneth Kumiega
Director of Training
Mazda Motor Manufacturing
 USA Corporation

Alan Ladhams
Vice-President
Polaroid Corporation

William Wiggenhorn
Director of Training
Motorola, Incorporated

Organization and Strategic Role Network

Nancy Adler
McGill University

Robert L. Anderson
Human Development Services

Eugene S. Andrews
General Electric Company

Sue Berryman
Columbia University

Mark Bieler
Bankers Trust

Veronica Biggins
C & S National Bank

Kermit Boston
Market Development and Training

Jack Bowsher
International Business Machines

Mary Broad
Defense Communications Agency

Judith K. Broida
The Johns Hopkins University

W. Warner Burke
W. Warner Burke & Associates

Christina Caron
British Embassy

Paul Chaddock
Lechmere, Inc.

Ivan Charner
National Institute for Work and
    Learning

Donald K. Conover
American Telephone and Telegraph

Louis B. DeAngelis
National Aeronautical and Space
    Administration

Russell Demers
Bristol Meyers

James D. DeVito
Johnson & Johnson

David Dotlich
Honeywell Bull

Michael Emmott
Manpower Services Commission

David Erhmann
Codex Corporation

Badi G. Foster
Aetna Institute for Corporate Education

John Fox
Los Alamos National Laboratory

Daryl Hall
New York Telephone

John Harper
Malta Development Corporation

G. Richard Hartshorn
Ford Motor Company

Howard A. Hayman
New England Telephone

William J. Hessler
The Upjohn Company

Gerald K. Hinch
U.S. Office of Personnel Management

Larry Hirschhorn
Wharton Center for Applied Research

Emily Huebner
The American University

John W. Humphrey
The Forum Corporation

Edie Hutton
Landmark Bancshares Corporation

Betsy Jaffe
Career Continuum

Glenn Jeffrey
Pillsbury Company

Mathew Juechter
Integration Resource Associates

Donald D. Kane
Cornell University

Deborah M. Kerr
Philadelphia National Bank

Jerry Kinnane
Advanced Technology

Maria Kontras
Hickey-Mitchell Company

Michael J. Kruger
U.S. Department of the Treasury

Kenneth Kumiega
Mazda Motor Manufacturing

Al Ladhams
Polaroid Corporation

Craig Lundberg
Cornell University

Christopher Lydon
Learning International

Robert McDowell
Coopers & Lybrand

James MacHulbert
Columbia University

Howard Mase
Citicorp

Karen L. Miller
Cardinal Glennon Children's Hospital

John Newstrom
University of Minnesota

Thierry Noyelle
Conservation of Human Resources

Dianne O'Connell
Harris Corporation

Susan C. Paddock
Arizona State University

Lymon Porter
University of California, Irvine

Edmund H. Rieger
Rockwell International Corporation

Veda Ross
St. Vincent Hospital

Lynda W. Rothman
Amoco Corporation

Elizabeth Benazer Rowley
Kellogg Community College

Thomas Sablo
Time-Life Books

Esther Sangster
Tampa General Hospital

Stephen Schlossberg
U.S. Department of Labor

Warren Schmidt
University of Southern California

Delores J. Schwenk
First Federal Savings and Loan
  Association

John Sims
Digital Equipment Corporation

Hyman Small
James River Corporation

Yvonne S. Sparks
Metropolitan St. Louis Sewer
  District

Leslie Krauz Stambaugh
RLS Associates

Edward E. Sutton
New York Telephone Company

Fred A. Swan
University of Massachusetts

Arty Trost
Organizational Dynamics

Jerry W. Unroe
Garland Floor

Edward Verlander
Salomon Brothers, Inc.

James Ray Watson
Fuqua School of Business

Jeffrey Wells
Toys R Us

Lana Wertz
Aetna Institute for Corporate
  Education

William Wiggenhorn
Motorola Training & Education

Jeff Willbur
Service Master Industries, Inc.

Richard E. Wise
The Travelers Corporation

William N. Yeomans
The Yeomans Group, Inc.

Training in America

PART 1

The Players:
Institutions, Employers, Trainees

CHAPTER 1

Who Provides Training

Whether upgrading current employees or preparing entry-level workers, employers and external education and training institutions are partners in the learning enterprise. Employers themselves provide 69 percent of the formal training they offer and buy the other 31 percent from outside providers. External education and training institutions range from elementary and secondary schools to apprenticeship programs. This chapter briefly describes the wide variety of institutions that work in partnership with employers. Table 1 presents an overview of outside provider contributions to the learning enterprise.

Table 1. Formal Training by Source.

Provider	Share of Purchased Training (Percent)	Dollar Value (Millions)
All schools	56.4	5,245.2
Elementary and secondary schools	1.5	139.5
Colleges and universities	31.2	2,901.6
Community colleges and technical institutes	15.5	1,441.5
Vocational schools	7.0	651.0
Other schools	1.2	111.6
Professional, trade, and labor organizations	14.2	1,320.0
Training industry	15.7	1,460.0
Community organizations	3.2	297.6
Tutors and private instructors	1.2	111.6
Government	5.6	520.0
Other	3.5	325.5

Source: U.S. Census Bureau, 1987.

3

The Education System

American schools serve three masters: American culture, the political system, and the economy. American culture values individualism above all else, and the American political system is predicated on participation. The schools are responsible for developing autonomous individuals who can contribute to the American community and participate in the American political system.

The economic role of the schools is pivotal. They are charged with husbanding and disseminating knowledge that will allegedly create the next technology and the next set of employers, jobs, and employees. However, under the current educational framework, the quantity and quality of jobs are essentially given, and, contrary to perception, education has only a marginal effect in creating jobs by making high-quality labor a better investment than machine capital. Therefore, the primary mission for schools is to educate for existing jobs by providing generic skills to make people ready for work and for learning on the job.

In 1985, 28.1 million workers (about 30 percent of the American work force) reported they had received some or all of their qualifying training from schools. Most (about 16.1 million workers) got their qualifying training from four-year postsecondary institutions. About 5 million got their jobs as a result of training at junior colleges or technical institutes. Another 5 million got some or all of their qualifying training in high school vocational education courses. Roughly 2 million qualified for their jobs as a result of training in private postsecondary vocational schools, and 1.5 million qualified as a result of training in public postsecondary vocational schools (Carey, 1985).

Elementary and Secondary Schools

The elementary and secondary school system is the largest component of the nation's education and training system. The nation's public and private elementary and secondary schools currently serve 40 million students at a cost of $150 billion per year.

Local, state, and federal governments spent more than $137 billion on public elementary and secondary schools for the 1984–85 school year. Although federal funding for elementary and secondary education is overshadowed by the contributions of state and local governments, which together accounted for about 94 percent of all funding in 1984–85, the federal government proposed $11.5 billion for educational programs in fiscal year 1988, including $5.1 billion for elementary and secondary school programming (U.S. Department of Education, 1988; U.S. Office of Management and Budget, 1987). That large public investment in education has had some gratifying results. The nation's secondary schools provide occupational education to about 5.5 million students at a cost of about $6.5 billion per year.

Arguably, the nation's schools are its most effective institution. As of October 1985, 86.5 percent of whites, 82.5 percent of blacks, and 70 percent of Hispanics had received a high school education. Overall, 86 percent of young adults ages twenty-five to twenty-nine were high school graduates, twice the percentage for 1940. The annual dropout rate fell from 6.3 percent in 1973 to 5.2 percent in 1983, with young black men showing the most improvement.

Despite these gains, there are considerable educational attainment gaps that exist, particularly among race and ethnic groups and various economic strata. Black and Hispanic teenagers are far more likely to leave school before graduating than are white youths, and poor youths, regardless of race or ethnic group, are three to four times more likely to drop out than students from higher-income families. In 1985, for the age range from eighteen to twenty-one, only 56 percent of blacks and 53 percent of whites from poor families had earned a high school degree. Hispanics at all economic levels are especially at risk for leaving school early (Wetzel, 1987).

Concern for the quality of schooling has moved beyond the traditional focus on the economically and educationally disadvantaged to concern for the schooling of all the nation's children. This broader interest was best expressed in a report by the U.S. Department of Education that warned dramatically that the educational foundations of American society are being eroded by a rising tide of mediocrity that threatens the nation's future (National Commission on Excellence in Education, 1983). So far, reforms have been on the right track by putting greater emphasis on improving basic academic skills (reading, mathematics, and the sciences); expanding the traditional curriculum to include the interpersonal, teamwork, and organizational skills needed in the workplace; improving the quality of teaching/training; and testing both teachers and students for subject competency attainment.

Of particular concern to education reformers is the quality of education available to general and vocational education students, who together make up about 61 percent of the high school student population. This "other half" of the high school graduating class appears to be receiving a poor basic skills education and outdated occupational preparation that ultimately limit their opportunities and effectiveness in the workplace. Reformers tend to agree that this population requires a new curriculum that integrates the basics with job-related learning.

Colleges and Universities

The college and university system prepares the nation's white-collar and technical professionals, including managers and specialists (see Chapter Three for discussion of occupational groups). The United States supports 156 universities and 1,853 colleges with a combined enrollment of almost 8 million students. These institutions spend almost $80 billion annually, or roughly $13,000 per student.

Twenty-two percent of all Americans in the age range from twenty-five to twenty-nine have completed four years of college, nearly double the percentage for 1963 and four times the percentage for 1940. Long-term relative educational gains for black youth have been even more dramatic than those for whites. The proportions of both high school and college graduates among black youth have risen sevenfold since 1940.

College and university graduates tend to keep their skills current, whether to meet certification or licensing requirements or to meet self-imposed standards of their professions or occupations. They rely more heavily on schooling to prepare for work than do other Americans. Their upgrading after employment comes from a mix of postgraduate education, the offerings of professional societies, and employer-sponsored training. Compared with other Americans, college and university graduates get the most preparation before they go to work and the most formal and informal training while they are on the job.

Colleges and universities provide more qualifying and upgrading training for Americans than all other schools combined. They provided qualifying training for 16.1 million persons and upgrading for 5.5 million persons in 1985 (Carey, 1985). But the economic importance of colleges and universities is not limited to their ability to teach and retrain Americans. Four-year institutions are also a principal source of the nation's research and development (R&D), which ultimately drives new innovations, skill change, and education and training requirements.

The importance of college education is not likely to decrease any time soon, given the importance of R&D and the fact that, with the exception of teachers, occupations requiring college degrees are the fastest growing. Moreover, as high school completion rates continue to increase, quality improvements in high school education and college and other forms of postsecondary education will be the principal means for leveraging the economic contributions of education in the United States.

Increasing college enrollments are caused by not only the large number of young people of college age but also an increase in the number of older students. Between 1972 and 1976, the proportion of students age twenty-five and older in four-year institutions rose from 28 to 33 percent of the total college population. Much of the increase is attributable to female college students over age thirty-five. Their number climbed from 418,000 in 1972 to 700,000 in 1976, a 67.5 percent increase. Enrollments for all persons age twenty-five and over increased 44.6 percent during this same period (U.S. Department of Education, 1987).

Although colleges and universities have long been involved in the education of adults through their continuing education and extension departments, the shift to an older student population has led to (or perhaps been partially caused by) a need for new options to accommodate students' changing requirements. Admissions and formal entry qualifications have been eased, classes are scheduled at times and places more convenient to working adults, radio and television have been used to transmit course material, and independent study has been encouraged. A few colleges and universities also provide credit for nontraditional learning experiences in various external degree programs.

Postsecondary Occupational Education

The postsecondary occupational education system is the principal system for preparing and upgrading the half of high school graduates who do not go on to college and who ultimately populate the nonsupervisory work force as technicians, technologists, and craft and skilled workers. Junior colleges, technical schools, vocational schools, the military, and employers are the principal providers of occupational education after high school.

Junior Colleges and Technical Institutes. Junior colleges and technical institutes are the foremost providers of qualifying training and upgrading in this system. According to the Bureau of Labor Statistics, junior colleges and technical institutes provided qualifying training for about 5 million workers and upgrading for 3.3 million workers in 1985 (Carey, 1985). These schools tend to provide job-related education for a highly motivated group of noncollege students (nurses, health technicians, electricians, computer technicians, and so on).

Junior colleges and technical institutes have become an increasingly important source of occupational training in communities across the United States. In 1933–34, there were only 532 two-year colleges nationwide, with an enrollment of just over 110,000; in 1983–84, the number of two-year institutions had risen to 1,219 and full-year enrollments to nearly 5 million. About 55 percent of all college freshmen were enrolled in community, technical, and junior colleges. Counting the estimated 4.5 million noncredit enrollees, total enrollments in junior colleges and other two-year institutions reached nearly 10 million in 1983–84. The average age of the student body is twenty-nine

(Fraser, 1980), a fact that reflects the attraction of community colleges for adult learners.

The appeal of these institutions to adult learners derives from a variety of factors, including affordable tuition and fees (an average of $600 in 1984–85 compared with more than $1,000 in universities and four-year colleges) (Parnell, 1985), liberal admission policies, accessibility (courses are frequently offered on site at businesses, union halls, and other off-campus areas), a wide range of course offerings, and flexibility of class scheduling (most schools are open from early morning to late evening). Flexible scheduling is especially important because a large percentage of both full-time and part-time students at these schools are employed while attending classes (Godfrey and Holmstrom, 1970).

Vocational Schools. Noncollegiate vocational schools provide job-related training in many of the same areas as junior colleges but tend to specialize in less-technical fields such as barbering, hairdressing, and truck driving. These institutions provided qualifying training for 3.7 million workers and upgrading for 1.6 million workers in 1985 (Carey, 1985).

Vocational institutions are the likely training vehicle for the growing mass of technicians in manufacturing and service industries, especially health care and financial services. These schools offer a relatively inexpensive alternative for human capital development beyond high school.

The Military. Military training accounts for the largest share of government training expenditures. For fiscal year (FY) 1989, $17.6 billion was appropriated to provide 249,168 "man years" of training to persons in all service branches (U.S. Department of Defense, 1988). The types of instruction offered included basic recruit training, officer preparation (Reserve Officers Training Corp [ROTC]), military academies (Officers Candidate School [OCS], and the like), medical training, professional development, and reserve training.

In addition to the basic and specialized training offered by the military, each service branch has cooperative arrangements with civilian schools to enable service personnel to earn high school diplomas or work toward college degrees. Several credit-by-examination and correspondence programs are also offered. Finally, the army, navy, and marine corps have developed registered apprenticeship programs that enable enrollees to receive credit for their service experience in civilian apprenticeship programs.

According to the Bureau of Labor Statistics, the military has provided qualifying training to almost two million Americans. Job-related training in the military is concentrated in electronics, computers, and aircraft engine repair (Carey, 1985).

The military uses distinctive training technologies and methods of delivery. Its principal contribution to the nation's learning enterprise is to develop training practices and technologies and to disseminate them to the civilian education and training institutions.

Formal Apprenticeship Programs

Formal apprenticeship programs, which now apply to some 415 trades, include both classroom instruction (a minimum of 144 hours a year) and hands-on learning (a minimum of 2,000 hours, or one year of on-the-job training [OJT]). Under the National Apprenticeship (Fitzgerald) Act of 1937, unions and employers determine their own requirements and administer their own training programs within the framework of basic standards laid down by state apprenticeship councils or the Bureau of Apprenticeship and Training, U.S. Department of Labor. If an apprenticeship program meets these standards, it is "registered," and persons who successfully complete the training receive certificates of completion that entitle them to the prerequisites of skilled craft workers.

Training periods range from one to six years depending on the degree of skill involved, with most trades requiring from three to four years of instruction. While apprentices train on the job, they are paid at progressive wage rates, starting at about half the journey-level rate and reaching up to 95 percent of full pay near the end of the apprenticeship period. Persons who complete programs are usually among the highest-paid skilled workers.

Usually, apprenticeship programs accept applications for only a few weeks each year, and the number of openings is limited. Application to an apprenticeship program generally requires a high school diploma or its equivalent, a written examination, and an oral interview. Despite efforts to lower perceived barriers to training for women and minorities, such as the Targeted Outreach Program, which was funded under the Comprehensive Employment and Training Act of 1972, the proportion of minorities and women enrolled in apprenticeships has never been high.

Technical instruction as a part of apprenticeship training is given in local vocational schools and junior colleges, and in some cases home study courses may also be accepted. Provisions of the Smith-Hughes (1917) and George-Barden (1946) Vocational Acts as well as the Vocational Education Act of 1963 have permitted states with approved apprenticeship programs to receive partial reimbursement from federal funds for salaries of teachers and vocational administrators.

In 1978 (the most recent data available) there were 395,000 registered apprentices receiving training, an increase of 33,000 over the previous year. More than 50,000 apprentices completed required training that year, and 131,000 were newly indentured (formally accepted as apprentices). As of December 31, 1978, slightly more than 60 percent of the registered apprentices in the country were in building trade occupations, nearly all of them in the unionized sector. Programs in three construction trades — carpentry, electrical, and the pipe trades — contained almost 40 percent of all registered apprentices (U.S. Department of Labor, 1987).

In concept, apprenticeship is the ideal job-related training program. It mixes academic and applied learning, allowing learners to support themselves while they learn. It is a way for employed workers to upgrade their skills and occupational standing while still on the job. It allows for an applied evaluation of curricula by testing or observing job performance. The principal difficulty with apprenticeship is its limited application among the nation's occupations and industries.

Second Chance Training

The second chance training system is composed of both public and nonprofit institutions that offer federally funded, locally delivered public programs to persons who are not receiving training from either the public schools or employers. It provides assistance for dropouts, persons who have failed or are likely to fail the transition from school to work, the underemployed, the working poor, and persons who have been dislocated from their jobs with dim prospects for reemployment. Almost forty million Americans currently fall into one or more of these categories. The second chance system performs a brokering function between its clients and employers, using small doses of education, training, and job search assistance to help the disadvantaged find work and access to learning on the job.

History. Since the early 1960s, the federal government has subsidized a variety of training programs aimed primarily at serving economically disadvantaged persons who have not benefited from early educational opportunities. Its effort began with the enactment of the Area Redevelopment Act (ARA) of 1961. ARA established a precedent for federally subsidized training offered in conjunction with loans to companies that agreed to relocate or expand industrial facilities into impoverished areas.

Although ARA never served more than 12,000 people in a year, it was quickly followed by the more ambitious Manpower Development and Training Act (MDTA) of 1962, which offered participants up to a year of skill training in the classroom or on the job. Originally, MDTA anticipated current concerns about the dislocating effects of technological change, directing its efforts to adult family heads who could demonstrate by their employment history a strong attachment to the labor force.

Soon after MDTA's enactment, however, demands for skilled workers increased to meet production needs associated with the Vietnam War, and unemployment levels for adult males dropped. In response, federal policy shifted to focus on the problems of poor youths and minorities, who continued to have high unemployment rates. The most important step in that direction was the enactment of the Economic Opportunity Act (EOA) of 1963, which was to become the cornerstone of President Johnson's War on Poverty.

Nearly half of EOA funding in the first year was for youth programs, including the Neighborhood Youth Corps (NYC) and the Job Corps. Both programs offered poor youths an opportunity to learn job skills. NYC did so by offering a program of part-time work experience, and the Job Corps by providing basic education and occupational skill training combined with an array of medical, dental, and other support services in a residential setting away from debilitating home environments. EOA also offered a small program for adults under Title V: it provided work experience, classroom training, and family services to the parents of dependent children on welfare.

Because EOA was reauthorized annually until 1967, frequent amendments to the act added new programs every year: Operation Mainstream (1965) provided elderly workers with part-time jobs in rural conservation projects, New Careers (1966) offered public-sector jobs to the economically disadvantaged, the Special Impact Program (1966) focused federal training dollars on selected urban slum areas, and the Concentrated Employment Programs (1967) created a new delivery system to provide a complete range of employment and training programs and related supportive services in targeted rural and urban areas with very high rates of unemployment.

MDTA was also amended several times in that period to reflect the new policy direction of serving poor youths. In 1967, by executive order, President Johnson created a new MDTA program called Job Opportunities in the Business Sector. The new program offered employers reimbursement for extra costs associated with hiring and training disadvantaged workers and established the National Alliance of Business to recruit employers for that effort.

The roster of new antipoverty programs was completed in 1967 with the authorization of the Work Incentive (WIN) program as an amendment to the Social Security Act. WIN was designed to provide training, supportive services, and job placement assistance to eligible recipients of Aid to Families with Dependent Children (AFDC).

Efforts to rationalize what had become an expensive array of separately funded programs began with the presidency of Richard Nixon in 1969. Although the president was resolved to decategorize those programs into a single block grant, shift administrative control to state and local governments, and cut expenditures, he first found himself bowing to the realities of a severe recession in 1970–71 by signing into law a $2.25-billion, two-year Public Employment Program under the Emergency Employment Act of 1971. With the addition of these funds, outlays for federal employment and training programs reached the level of $5 billion in FY 1973. Legislators, policymakers, and the president were at last in general agreeement that it was time to reform the federal employment and training system, although they did not agree on what form a new system might take.

The Comprehensive Employment and Training Act (CETA) of 1973 was the end product of this struggle. As finally enacted, this compromise legislation provided for a comprehensive program of training and related services for the economically disadvantaged, a program of transitional public service employment for the most severely disadvantaged and for eligible veterans in areas of very high unemployment, special federal training programs for Native Americans and migrant and seasonal farm workers, a reauthorization of the Job Corps, and a National Commission for Manpower Policy to make recommendations about meeting the employment needs and goals of the nation. The new law gave local prime sponsors broad authority to develop programs tailored to community needs, and CETA training programs, which were meant to be the central focus of the new legislation, paid stipends at least equal to the minimum wage.

Although designed as a training program, CETA was soon overwhelmed by its public job creation activities in response to a deep nationwide recession prompted in part by the OPEC oil embargo. Responding to congressional pressure, President Ford reluctantly agreed to a new Emergency Jobs Program, which became a new title under CETA in 1974. This was in addition to the public service job creation program already a part of CETA and, together with the two public job creation titles, soon accounted for more than half of all CETA outlays. Shortly before the presidential election of 1976, President Ford agreed to an extension of the Emergency Jobs Program but balked at any further increase in funds.

The Carter administration did not share that reluctance and called for an expansion from 300,000 to 750,000 job slots over a nine-month period in 1977. Youth employment initiatives were a major goal of the Carter administration, which established a vice-president's task force on youth and a special youth office in the Department of Labor to oversee several new programs authorized by the Youth Employment and Demonstration Projects Act (YEDPA) of 1977.

Amendments to other legislation added two new programs offering tax credits to employers who expanded their work force by hiring poor youths and other groups with special needs. Those credits were the New Jobs Tax Credit of 1977, a $4-billion program not restricted to the disadvantaged, and the Targeted Jobs Tax Credit of 1978, more specifically targeted on disadvantaged groups enumerated in the act.

The final revision of CETA took place in 1978 with several amendments designed to improve program management and CETA's public image. These amendments included limitations on the discretionary authority of local and state governments, changes in public service employment eligibility requirements to target only the poor, and the development of a new private-sector initiative program to bring representatives from private businesses into partnership with local elected officials in planning and administering programs. Those revisions were not enough to silence critics of the program, however.

In 1983, after a one-year period of transition from CETA, the Reagan administration began the implementation of the Job Training Partnership Act (JTPA) (passed in 1982), which provided a basic program of training services for disadvantaged youths and adults, a program of retraining and job search assistance for dislocated workers, and the continuation of the Job Corps, and a number of federally administered programs for Native Americans and migrant and seasonal farm workers.

JTPA gives states much of the oversight authority once reserved for the federal government, and private industry councils (PICs), composed mainly of business leaders, are in equal partnership with local elected officials for administering local programs. Public service employment is prohibited under the act, and work experience is severely limited. Stipends for participants are not permitted, although needs-based allowances and supported services can be offered up to the limit imposed by the 30 percent restriction on administrative and support service costs.

Current Second Chance System. The history of the second chance system demonstrates a steadily increasing involvement of employers. Because early experience showed that learning outside the context of a job or a real job prospect had little positive effect on improving employment, legislative changes have progressively attempted to strengthen the relationship between the second chance system and employers.

The current demography has created a window of opportunity for the second chance system. The declining quantity of entry-level employees has created common cause between the second chance system and employers. As entry-level employees become more and more scarce, more and better jobs become available to the disadvantaged and dislocated workers who are clients of the second chance system. The emerging strength of this system stems from the fact that its goals of opportunity and social justice are increasingly consistent with the public and private pursuit of the nation's economic competitiveness.

The principal programs that make up the second chance system are funded primarily under the JTPA and also under the WIN program, part of the Aid to Families with Dependent Children (AFDC) Act. The JTPA has now been in operation for several years and emphasizes public-private partnerships, performance standards, coordination of training services with other human service agencies, state and local administrative control, and access to work and career development rather than welfare.

The Career Support System

The emerging career support system is a set of experimental policies and programs that are loosely connected by a common intention to give employees and their families more control over their working lives. On the whole, this system represents a profound shift in the focus of the national dialogue on human resource development: the public interest in developing human capital has moved beyond an exclusive concern for the disadvantaged to a new focus on the mainstream working population.

Americans are learning from the demoralizing example of dislocated workers that competition intensifies economic and technical change, requiring a more flexible work force and loosening the ties between employer and employee. Most Americans believe that they now have diminished job security and must take more responsibility for their own career development. They also believe that in order to shoulder this new responsibility, they will need a bag of new tools, including involvement in economic and technical changes that affect them at work; access to retraining to help them keep pace with economic and technical change; and portable health care, day care, parental leave, and pensions to sustain them and their families on and off the job.

Thus far, the emerging career support system is more dream than reality. It consists of training and other labor market services in collective bargaining agreements and limited public experimentation with training provisions for employed adults.

It is difficult to judge the future of the career support system. The services involved are expensive, and the federal government has insufficient resources to afford them. If costs are foisted on private employers, they will have less investment capital available, and individual jobs will be so expensive that employers will be unable to hire as many full-time workers as they might otherwise hire.

Public and Private Employment Agencies. Probably the oldest transitional institution in the United States is the system of public employment agencies. Since the 1930s, the principal provider of publicly supported job search assistance has been the U.S. Employment Service (or Job Service, as it is now called in most states). The Job Service is a federally funded, state-administered system, with approximately 2,600 offices operating throughout the country.

Under the terms of the Wagner-Peyser Act of 1933, anyone who is legally qualified to work in the United States is entitled to receive, without charge, services that range from aptitude testing and vocational counseling to job development and placement. Each year, about sixteen million people seek help through local Job Service offices, and about six million job openings are filled. Additional services such as job analysis, studies of turnover and absenteeism, and assistance in job restructuring are offered to employers along with help in filling their job openings. Finally, the Job Service has a major recruitment role for several federal employment and training programs such as JTPA and WIN.

In contrast to the public employment service, which must by law accept all job seekers regardless of skill or aptitude, private employment agencies often specialize in particular fields and prescribe the level of education or other characteristics required of applicants. The number of private agencies, which include large, nationwide temporary help firms as well as exclusive executive search agencies, appears to have increased substantially over time. Although the exact number of agencies cannot be determined, one estimate is that there are approximately 17,000 private employment agencies and 1,100 executive search firms throughout the country (Johnston, 1987).

In addition to activities that relate directly to job placement, there are a number of other programs, both public and

private, designed to provide young people in particular but other
entry-level workers as well with the experience they need to find
career paths that suit their personal needs. Some of these programs offer career information and counseling, others provide
work experience through internships or preemployment training, and still others offer incentives to continue education or
training (Johnston, 1987).

Examples of these various programs are discussed in the
following three sections.

Occupational and Career Information. In addition to providing job placement services through local Job Service offices,
the federal government funds programs to help people make
informed choices about career decisions. For example, the National Occupational Information Coordinating Committee
(NOICC) and its counterpart state committees (SOICCs) are
authorized under the Vocational Education Act. NOICC,whose
members are officials of the Department of Labor and the Department of Education, is responsible for coordinating federal,
state, and local efforts to improve occupational and career information activities at all levels of government.

Among the projects NOICC has funded is the Career Information System grants program, which uses a multimedia approach (computers, microfiche, and printed material) to provide
information about occupations and careers. A number of states
have used this prototype to develop occupational information
systems of their own, using state and local funding (Johnston,
1987; William T. Grant Foundation, 1988, p. 43).

Jobs for America's Graduates (JAG) is an effort designed
to assist high school students in making their way into the job
market. Currently operating in twelve states, the program serves
approximately 11,000 students who have been identified as
potential dropouts. JAG offers instruction in career planning,
job-seeking skills, personal development, and other work-related
skills as well as job development and placement assistance provided by professional job specialists and membership in a student career association. Follow-up support is provided for nine
months after graduation (William T. Grant Foundation, 1988,
pp. 42, 43).

Internship Programs. The Career Intern Program, developed by the Opportunities Industrialization Council in Philadelphia with financial support from the National Institute of Education, is another example of preemployment assistance directed specifically at dropouts or potential dropouts. Participants receive a combination of classroom instruction oriented toward occupations and supervised work experience accompanied by career counseling and social services, which continues for six months to a year after participants have either found jobs or continued their education.

Similar kinds of internship programs not directed exclusively to youths at risk include New York City's Executive High School Internship program and the National Institute of Education's model Experience-Based Career Education (EBCE) program. Teacher-coordinators supervise placements and lead seminars to reinforce what is learned. In the New York City program, youngsters are paired with executives, who act as role models and provide career information. EBCE participants change placements frequently to get a wide range of experience in both blue-collar and white-collar jobs (National Alliance of Business, 1988).

Incentive Programs. Some programs designed to provide preemployment experience and career information also offer incentives to remain in school. One of the best-known programs, the Boston Compact Project, which began in 1982, is an effort to bring together the resources of the public schools and the business, university, and labor communities to improve students' academic achievement and work preparation. The compact, as its name implies, is a formal, objective-based agreement that stipulates the contributions each entity will make to improve educational performance, school attendance, and post–high school opportunities.

In 1982, Boston public schools had a 16 percent annual dropout rate, with less than 60 percent of any entering high school class remaining long enough to graduate. Under the terms of the compact, the schools agreed to reduce the dropout rate by 5 percent annually and to work toward increases in attendance and test scores. Businesses agreed to give priority hiring status to a specific number of graduates, to increase the number of summer jobs for students, and to sign up at least two hundred companies for a priority hiring effort. The compact was later expanded to include colleges, which agreed to increase their enrollment rate among Boston public school graduates by 25 percent, and labor unions, which pledged openings in apprenticeship programs to graduates on the condition that the schools offer union-designed training curricula.

Currently, two initiatives are under way to address the dropout problem in Boston. First, the school system is attempting to create a dropout prevention plan that will bring in community resources and deal with structural barriers to school retention. Second, Compact Ventures, a pilot program sponsored by the Boston Private Industry Council in cooperation with the schools, offers supportive services and employment incentives to high-risk ninth-graders in two schools.

The Boston Compact has generally been considered a success, although it has proven most adept at increasing the employment of high school graduates. About one-third of the graduating class of 1986 found jobs through the compact, many in banks, insurance companies, and hospitals, at wages that averaged $5.43 per hour. Some progress has also been made in improving attendance and academic achievement, but the dropout rate remains unchanged. The Boston economy has been thriving in recent years, and it is open to question whether the compact will prove equally effective in a slower labor market.

Building on the compact's strengths, seven other cities (Albuquerque, Cincinnati, Indianapolis, Louisville, Memphis, San Diego, and Seattle) have also initiated similar projects, tailored to their individual communities, as part of a nationwide demonstration program. Funding for the seven projects is supervised by the National Alliance of Business and is provided by the U.S. Department of Labor and Department of Health and Human Services, along with grants from the Reader's Digest Foundation and the MacArthur Foundation. Each participating city is working toward implementing formal, written compacts between public schools and business, government, and higher education. The agreements will specify overall goals for each city and assign responsibility for attaining those goals to the various parties to the agreements.

New York businessman Eugene Lang, who "adopted" a sixth-grade class in East Harlem, has guaranteed those children funding for college or other continuing education. Business philanthropists have followed suit in Boston, Dallas, the District of Columbia, and other communities around the country. Although dependent on the goodwill of wealthy individuals, such programs offer hope to young people who remain in school and prepare for postsecondary education and training.

The Training Industry

The training industry provides training tailored to the needs of specific employers. Large companies buy almost 40 percent of their formal training from outside providers, mid-sized employers buy an even larger share, and small employers go outside for nearly all their formal training.

The training industry is multifaceted. Since its primary characteristic is to provide training based on the special needs of an employer, the training industry includes all those institutions and businesses that assume that training role. Therefore, the training industry includes institutions that provide primarily upgrading training: vendors and consultants, educational institutions, community-based organizations, corporations that sell their training programs, professional and trade associations, unions, and governments. (See Chapter Five for an in-depth discussion of the training industry.)

CHAPTER 2

How the Employer-Based Training System Works

Learning on the job is nothing new. Two out of three Americans say that everything they need to know to do their jobs was learned on the job — not through classroom preparation to qualify for those jobs.

The workplace is the most frequently traveled avenue to education and training for most employed persons. It is a large and growing player in the nation's learning enterprise. Estimates of employer investment in workplace training hover around $210 billion annually. About $30 billion, or 1 to 2 percent of employers' payrolls, is estimated to be spent on formal training, while another $180 billion annually is invested in informal, or on-the-job, training.

Employer-provided training can take many forms. It may be available as formalized instruction in a classroom setting, designed and delivered lecture style by in-house training staff. It may be delivered via interactive video or through other computerized instruction systems. Employer-provided formalized training may mean that an employer has contracted with an outside training provider (consultant) to design, develop, and deliver training either on or off the employer's worksite.

Employer-provided training also comes as on-the-job training. It may be structured, such as that provided through apprenticeship programs. It may be unstructured and as informal as coaching — as straightforward as one person's showing another the best way to perform an assigned task.

The obvious costs of the employer investment in training are small, however, when we explore the notion that whenever people are working, they are learning. In fact, it is very
hard to draw the line between performing a task or job and ac-
cumulating knowledge about that task or job. Any labor economist can argue that learning on the job is constant and deduce
that the total payroll of the American work force is an investment in workplace learning. With that reasoning, America's investment in employer-provided training would top $2.7 trillion
per year!

History

Through the centuries humans have conducted informal
training. What the British call "sitting next to Jenny," or learning by doing, is a time-honored training approach.

Formalized training can trace its early roots to apprenticeships, where novice craftsmen studied under experts who
shared years of knowledge and experience in their craft. As early
as 1800 B.C. the Babylonian Code of Hammurabi laid out rules
governing the transferring of skills from one generation to another, from artisans to youth. The earliest Egyptian, Grecian,
and Roman historical records also discuss the formalized passing of craft knowledge from masters to apprentices (U.S. Department of Labor, 1987, p. 2).

During the Middle Ages, training became more structured and systematic when trade guilds were formed. Guilds
brought together individuals with an interest or expertise in a
common craft. "There were three classes of membership in
guilds: master workers, who owned the raw materials and tools,
and directed the work; apprentices, who usually lived with the
master and who received practically no pay except for maintenance and training; and journeymen, who had passed through
the apprenticeship stage but were not yet qualified as masters"
(Miller, 1987, p. 5).

When Europeans colonized America, they brought with
them the system of master-apprenticeship relationships. This
system meant the difference between the colonies' relying solely
on the Old World for goods and services and their independence.

Through the development of a cadre of skilled craftsmen, the New World became self-sufficient.

Training on the job took a giant step forward with the advent of the industrial revolution in the late eighteenth century. "The early system of 'domestic apprenticeship' in which an apprentice lived with a master and was dependent upon the master for food and clothing, disappeared. Compensation was changed by employers to the payment of wages" (U.S. Department of Labor, 1987, p. 9). Faced with a supply of former farm workers and schoolgirls who came to factory towns to find a new life, companies began to prepare workers for the life of the factory. By the mid 1800s, training in production processes was provided in the workplace as on-the-job training, the education system was enlisted to begin preparing people to enter the world of work through "vocational education," and some companies even launched "factory training schools" to provide formalized, classroom instruction (Miller, 1987, pp. 7–8).

In the late 1800s, the YMCA began offering education courses to help individuals qualify for craft jobs. Some higher educational institutions expanded their curricula and even launched schools that prepared workers for technical work in industrial settings. Cooperative education, where an employee would balance training and practical experience by working part time and attending school part time, was born at the University of Cincinnati's College of Engineering (Miller, 1987, p. 9).

Companies focused hard on training in the early 1900s, when Ford Motor introduced the assembly line concept, creating the need for specialized production workers. World War I fueled investment in training as the nation geared up its war machine — and found that a well-trained work force was the key to making factories produce the volume of products needed with the limited manpower available (Miller, 1987, p. 10).

During the 1920s immigration restrictions were imposed, and fewer skilled craftsmen entered the country. In addition, existing methods for training skilled technical workers caused a wide variance in the quality of workers. In response to this situation, national groups representing employers, organized labor, educators, and the U.S. government began exploring ways to ensure that a steady stream of qualified craftsmen entered the work force. Eventually, this coalition effort resulted in the passage of the National Apprenticeship Act of 1937, which created a formalized registration system for apprenticeship and the modern apprenticeship agreement (U.S. Department of Labor, 1987, pp. 2, 9, 16). The act is shown in Exhibit 1.

**Exhibit 1. The National Apprenticeship Act
(50 Stat. 663; 29 U.S.C. 50).**

To enable the Department of Labor to formulate and promote the furtherance of labor standards necessary to safeguard the welfare of apprentices and to cooperate with the States in the promotion of such standards.

Be it enacted by the Senate and House of Representatives of the United States of America in Congress assembled, That the Secretary of Labor is hereby authorized and directed to formulate and promote the furtherance of labor standards necessary to safeguard the welfare of apprentices, to extend the application of such standards by encouraging the inclusion thereof in contracts of apprenticeship, to bring together employers and labor for the formulation of programs of apprenticeship, to cooperate with State agencies engaged in the formulation and promotion of standards of apprenticeship, and to cooperate with the National Youth Administration and with the Office of Education of the Department of the Interior in accordance with section 6 of the Act of February 23, 1917 (39 Stat. 932), as amended by Executive Order Numbered 6166, June 10, 1933, issued pursuant to an Act of June 30, 1932 (47 Stat. 414), as amended.

Sec. 2. The Secretary of Labor may publish information relating to existing and proposed labor standards of apprenticeship, and may appoint national advisory committees to serve without compensation. Such committees shall include representatives of employers, representatives of labor, educators, and officers of other executive departments, with the consent of the head of any such department.

Sec. 3. On and after the effective date of this Act the National Youth Administration shall be relieved of direct responsibility for the promotion of labor standards of apprenticeship as heretofore conducted through the division of apprentice training and shall transfer all records and papers relating to such activities to the custody of the Department of Labor. The Secretary of Labor is authorized to appoint such employees as he may from time to time find necessary for the administration of this Act, with regard to existing laws applicable to the appointment and compensation of employees of the United States: *Provided, however,* That he may appoint persons now employed in the division of apprentice training of the National Youth Administration upon certification by the Civil Service Commission of their qualifications after nonassembled examinations.

Sec. 4. This Act shall take effect on July 1, 1937, or as soon thereafter as it shall be approved.

Approved, August 16, 1937.

With the Depression of the 1930s, many skilled people found themselves without jobs; throughout the Depression years, their skills, like unused machinery, were allowed to decay. As the country began to gear up for World War II, the skills deficit of American industry was clear—and the need for retraining was recognized. National leaders realized that many factory workers would go off to war, and replacements would have to be rapidly assimilated into the factories. The challenge would be twofold: to develop skilled line workers and to create a cadre of supervisory personnel who had the coaching and training skills essential for motivating the work force. "Suddenly, the training function of the supervisor became paramount. In fact, management found that without training skills, supervisors were unable to produce adequately for the war effort. With it, new records were being established by industrially inexperienced, handicapped and women workers" (Miller, 1987, p. 11).

In 1940, the National Defense Advisory Commission established the Training Within Industry Service (TWI) to assist defense industries in meeting their manpower needs through training. TWI was staffed by volunteers on loan from industry, full or part time; it provided consulting, advisory, and clearinghouse training services. In its first bulletin, TWI stated, "The underlying purpose of this activity is to assist defense industries to meet their manpower needs by training within industry each worker to make the fullest use of his best skill up to the maximum of his individual ability. . . . It is the intention of this organization to render specific advisory assistance to defense industries in inaugurating programs which they will carry on within their own plants at their own expense" (Kirkpatrick, 1973). Using employees to the maximum skill level involved three components basic to today's training industry: skills inventory, training outside of industry, and on-the-job training.

In the course of its existence, TWI was transferred and housed within four federal agencies. In 1942 President Franklin Roosevelt made the final transfer of TWI by placing it in the War Manpower Commission's Bureau of Training. By the time TWI shut down in 1945, it had trained 23,000 people as trainers

(Miller, 1987, p. 12). It had also ensured the establishment of a new profession — the training director.

The next three decades saw increased sophistication of training methodologies and management. Training became an institutionalized function of employer operations. Educators began to play a prominent role in providing the base learning for skilled workers, as community colleges and other institutions designed curricula in response to employer needs. New technologies led to new training delivery methods such as videotape and computer-assisted training. The professionalization of trainers inside and outside companies continued as attention focused on evaluation methods and calculating return on investment for training expenditures.

And the employer interest in training grew.

Snapshot: Learning in the Workplace

Learning systems in the workplace are the first line of defense against economic and technical changes. The ability of the nation's employers and employees to respond expeditiously to these changes determines, in large part, the nation's adaptability and competitiveness.

The employer's interest in employee education and training is utilitarian. It revolves around the core concern that new information and skills be readily applicable to employee responsibilities in the workplace. Employers recognize the importance of general academic education as a foundation for the acquisition and building of skills that contribute to the employer's business goals. However, employers also know that to be competitive, they must accelerate learning and integrate it rapidly. Therefore, designing and implementing training directly supportive of the employer's institutional culture and strategic goals take precedence over broad-based courses unconnected to the employer's central agenda.

The employer's ultimate goal in providing workplace learning opportunities is to improve the company's competitive advantage. Employers are therefore driven to identify and use learning approaches that rarely stray from the day-to-day reality of the workplace and are linked to both the individual on the job and, ultimately, the employer's bottom line. More cost-effective than broad-based training, this tailored, or "applied," approach provides training that responds to the employer's specific needs and triggers rapid integration of learning with actual job requirements, resulting in higher employee productivity.

Research and experience in adult learning have shown that linking learning to a worker's actual job pays off for employees as well. They are more likely to retain information provided in the context of their work because they will immediately and repeatedly use the newly acquired knowledge. Learning in the context of the workplace is frequently easier for employees than were their earlier experiences in academia. Applied learning is, by its very nature, more flexible than academic learning. Applied learning is facilitated by the very applicability of what trainees learn and the knowledge that the new learning will be used immediately and repeatedly on the job. In addition, workplace learning is supported by a powerful motivator: when learning experiences are based on actual job needs, employees frequently work to increase their proficiency in the expectation that they will trigger immediate rewards in terms of achievement, status, and earnings.

Employers and employees are, therefore, jointly motivated to make the workplace learning experience a success. The use of the applied learning method is growing toward that goal.

Applied Learning: The Common Thread

Although employees have always learned on the job, the employer-based training process has changed substantially in form. The fundamental dynamic has been a consistent shift from informal to formal learning. As the pace of economic and technical changes has accelerated over the past half century, employers have tried to ensure the efficiency and quality of learning by formalizing informal learning processes. Out of this have come efforts to link learning and real jobs by applying a careful methodology that translates real-world learning needs into structured learning programs.

This methodology is the "applied approach" to constructing workplace learning programs. It begins with a careful analysis of the difference between job requirements and employees'
current skills and ends with an evaluation of employees' performance on the job.

Pragmatic, work-based, and systematic, the applied approach has at its heart two basic tenets:

- Employers view skill deficiencies as barriers to productivity
  and marketplace success. Therefore, the employer's primary
  concern is to fill the gap between what employees know and
  what they need to know to improve job performance.
- The best method for improving job performance is to approach training needs systematically.

The systematic dimension of the applied approach has its
roots in seminal work by the United States military on what
it called Instructional Systems Design (ISD). Over the years
variations on the ISD theme have evolved. Systematic approaches
have many names, but they all include five stages: analysis of
training needs, design of training curriculum, development of
training curriculum, implementation (delivery), and evaluation.

This multistage process is dynamic, and the stages are
interactive like the changing patterns of a kaleidoscope. All stages
exert a significant and continual influence throughout the training process. Obviously, at various points throughout the process, one stage or other will inevitably dominate. Throughout,
however, all stages provide an undercurrent of influence. For
example, results of a needs assessment will inevitably undergo
rethinking as new knowledge is acquired during design and
implementation. Evaluation of training effects on actual job performance will invariably test and challenge not only the training program design and implementation but also the
interpretation of the original needs assessment.

In the mid 1980s many employers, spurred by competitive
pressures that redefined many marketplaces, moved to eliminate
training programs that did not directly contribute to their strategic agenda. As employers moved to leaner operations, train-

ing programs generally followed suit. However, unlike past trimmings, some recent approaches have focused not on a wholesale cutting of the training function but on a pruning and reshaping.

Influenced by the cost-effectiveness of ISD, many employers have restructured their training programs around the systematic approach. Gone is the vast array of broadly constructed courses available to the work forces of General Electric, Xerox, and IBM, to name a few. Instead, employers report a major reorientation toward needs-driven education and training and a move away from providing a patchwork of unconnected training courses covering topics recognized as "nice to know" but not immediately germane to the jobs at hand.

Training Systems: Structure and Organization

The training function in employer organizations is structured so that it is controlled centrally, decentrally, or through a combination of approaches.

In its purest sense, centralizing the training function means that all critical decisions affecting training, from expenditures through design, development, delivery, and evaluation, are controlled at a central decision point—usually at the headquarters of the employer organization.

Decentralizing the training function means that the organization has made a conscious decision to have all critical decisions affecting training controlled at the local or plant level of the organization. However, decentralization may also mean that training decisions are made in each operational division or unit and that there is no central coordinative decision point for managing training selections and expenditures.

In reality, most organizations have a blend of centralized and decentralized management of the training function. The landscape is ever changing, like shifting sands in a desert. In the 1970s and early 1980s, decentralization seemed to be a trend that many organizations adopted. In the mid 1980s, however, many organizations have returned to centralized control of training, at least in some sectors such as high-tech manufacturing. This is primarily because technology is changing so rapidly that successful training and learning are only possible if communication is a two-way street. The worker closest to the point of production or point of sale is most familiar with current technology and processes; any new training must reflect familiarity with the current vagaries of the system before successful integration of new training can occur. Therefore, in a dynamic environment where the only constant is change, training can only be effective if it is designed with the input of those closest to the line.

Trends

The trends seen among employer institutions do not present so much a clear picture of where and how training is controlled as unclear snapshots of a swirling landscape buffeted by the winds of necessity.

However, there appear to be three dominant scenarios. One snapshot shows training design and development controlled centrally but delivered decentrally to the plant level. Another shows training such as executive development, management development, and organization development being designed, developed, and delivered centrally but technical and skills training in the same organization being entirely decentralized. Still another shows operational units with the authority to make training decisions and purchases (decentralized) but with the requirement that a central training department participate in the training selection process or even approve that selection.

While these are the three most dominant patterns, employers can and do employ many variations and combinations. The position and management of the training function within employer institutions are influenced by economics, organizational politics, external factors such as regulatory requirements, and the competitive life cycle of individual products.

The financial health of an organization influences how much that organization allocates for training and the priority level it assigns to the management of the training function. These, in turn, may influence control decisions. External economic factors such as the fiscal health of the geographical region or regions in which the company operates may also drive control decisions—just as the national economic picture may affect these decisions.

Internal organizational politics may also influence how training is controlled. Control of the training function may be determined by the power of the executive charged with managing it and by how well leveraged that executive is within the organization. Moreover, the very welfare of and institutional commitment to training may be affected by the perspective of the organization's chief executive officer.

External environmental factors can play a role in the centralization/decentralization decision. When training is driven by regulatory requirements (as in the case of safety or hazardous waste disposal training), organizations frequently elect for centralized management to minimize potential legal complications arising from questions of noncompliance.

Lastly, the life cycle of a product may influence decisions concerning how training is controlled. The competitive cycle is the process by which innovations are developed and brought to the marketplace. The cycle can usually be divided into four phases:

1. Discovering or developing an innovation, such as a cost saving, quality improvement, or new product or service
2. Tailoring the innovation to the employer's institutional culture, strategic niche, and production or service delivery system
3. Utilizing the innovation in production or delivery of the new product or service to the marketplace
4. Developing new applications for the innovation

Training decisions affecting the discovery and development phase may need to be centralized, since the product concept is new and relatively few will have expert knowledge of the innovation to share. There will probably be a lack of clarity concerning the roles and responsibilities of employees, and assignments are likely to overlap. Training during this phase is likely to be both experimental and informal. Therefore, centralizing training decisions will minimize confusion and ensure controlled flow of correct information within the changing environment of this phase.

The tailoring phase demands a blend of centralization and decentralization. Centralized control may be required for executive and management development as well as organization development, because this phase may mean modifications in basic structures such as institutional culture and strategic direction. Training in new production or service delivery systems might be designed and developed at headquarters but delivered at local plant sites. During this phase, the employer has a clearer picture of what employees need to learn to integrate the innovation and is better able to define roles and responsibilities. Focus is on the information imparted and the quality of learning. At this phase, only marginal adjustments will be made; therefore, the organization can confidently formalize its training content and decentralize its delivery.

When the innovation becomes part of the production or delivery system, decentralization of training seems logical. During this phase, a circle of learning is created. Basic learning about the innovation has occurred, and continued learning is taking place at the point of production or point of sale. Marginal changes and efficiencies emerge, and information about them is fed back up the line. More control over learning is assumed by supervisors and line workers.

The Japanese have captured the essence of this phase in many ways by promoting a culture of the worker as "idea generator." Quality circles, for example, where workers join together to discuss current problems and new solutions, are critical to the circle of learning essential to the innovation phase of the product life cycle.

Eventually, this informal learning becomes formalized. A central decision point then disseminates the training that came from the bottom up. It is important to note, however, that any training that prepares employees to search for new applications must be embedded in the culture of the organization, so that whether training is centralized or decentralized, the learning circle continues.

When asked if training should be centralized or decentralized, most employers will answer either yes or no. Their choices are determined by circumstance and the dynamic interaction of economics, politics, legal requirements, and the competitive cycle.

Centralize or Decentralize: The Decision-Making Process

In the past, employers focused on decentralized training — independently operated, unique, customized programs directed toward specific sites or segments of a business. However, today's research indicates a turn toward centralized control for companywide generic training and decentralized control for technical, job-specific training. Research also indicates that centralized training is especially critical to organizations that are highly regulated, whose products must meet exacting standards, or for which safety is a critical factor of production because:

- Controlling training design and development at a central location avoids duplication and reduces training capital expenditures.
- Coordinating training development expands the training base, and employees at all facilities learn from the experience of each.
- Centralizing control ensures consistent training quality across large organizational segments, thus impacting cost effectiveness at a time when human capital is variable and both cash assets and physical plants are relatively fixed.

Regardless of where training is controlled, when top management prescribes an integral role for training, training activity increases throughout the organization and strengthens the centralized training function. Centralized training as a strategic tool for management usually occurs when employers want to:

- Implement change throughout the company.
- Address new innovations and technologies — a new product, strategy, or technology may require training large groups of employees as quickly and consistently as possible. Therefore, employers tend to provide centrally controlled training in the initial stages of innovations. Once innova-

tions are in place, however, training tends to become decentralized to fit the specific purposes of divisions and individual job categories.

- Convey specific institutional techniques or strategies — sales marketing personnel as well as customer service training tend to be organized around specific products or strategic units at the divisional level.
- Quickly and cost-effectively (economies of scale) deliver a standardized message.

Decisions to centralize or decentralize training are organization specific. There are no absolutes in the development and delivery of employer-based training. What works for one organization may not transfer to another. The method selected for development and delivery of training depends on an organization's fiscal resources, training mission, employee pool, training facilities, trainer resources, and strategic goals.

In addition, development and delivery are two separate issues and should be addressed as such. Centrally developed training is often decentrally delivered. For example, a national organization centrally develops an executive training program to educate managers on corporate management practices. Executives at each branch within the organization must receive training. The core program is distributed to branch offices, and each branch tailors and delivers the training program according to its operational goals.

Given organizational differences, companies should consider the following issues to determine whether to centralize or decentralize training development and delivery.

I.   Development Issues
   A.   Is the training new and not currently available in the institution?
   B.   Is the company trying to make a change in the institutional culture?
   C.   Is the training job specific?
   D.   Is the company trying to ensure institutional consistency through training?

    E. Is the training specific to isolated geographical or demographic conditions?

    F. Does the training need to reach a large population quickly?

    G. Must the training be embedded in the interchange between employee and the task?

    H. Does the training need to cross institutional boundaries?

    I. Is the training trying to quickly meet a technological advance?

II. Delivery Issues

    A. Does the organization have a centralized training facility?

    B. Is the training tailored to the employer location?

    C. How much time can employees be off the job to receive training?

    D. To what degree does training depend on technical equipment?

    E. Does the organization have in-house trainer capabilities?

Centralized training patterns vary and can take on many forms within an employer institution. Training can be centrally developed and centrally delivered by location, population, or function. Many large corporations centrally develop and deliver training, particularly management training, by location. For example, Motorola operates a training facility in Schaumburg, Illinois; Exxon has one in Florham Park, New Jersey; and Aetna has one in Hartford, Connecticut. The following examples illustrate centralized training structures organized by population and function that are used by corporations today.

Centralization by Population: Ford Motor Company. Ford Motor Company is one of the "Big Three" U.S. automakers. The company also manufactures trucks, farm equipment, aerospace systems and equipment, communications equipment, and electronic systems. In 1986 Ford reported $62.716 billion in sales. Ford's eleven divisions and numerous subsidiaries employ 382,300 individuals nationwide. Training and development play a major role in effecting both the cultural and the technological changes at Ford Motor Company. To accomplish cultural shift, Ford implemented centralized and decentralized training programs for salaried and hourly workers to learn how to work together more efficiently and productively.

Ford established a centralized Executive Development Center after a study showed that top executives were isolated from each other and that training was needed to incorporate the teamwork strategy necessary to manage the company through 1990. The Executive Development Center reports directly to the office of the chief executive. All center programs illustrate the impact of team versus isolationist activity to help executives abdicate group loyalty in favor of companywide perspectives. By mid 1987 the successful Executive Development Center offered training to more than fourteen hundred mid- and senior-level managers and was authorized to double its operating budget.

Centralization by Function: The Carrier Corporation. Carrier Corporation is a wholly owned subsidiary of United Technologies Corporation (UTC), an international company that designs and manufactures high-tech products such as Pratt & Whitney engines, Otis elevators, and Carrier air conditioners. Carrier, part of United Technology's building group, employs 33,000 workers and reported sales of $2.8 billion in 1986.

Carrier uses centralized technical training as a strategic tool. Because its products must meet exacting standards, and safety is a critical factor of production, Carrier's technical training directly supports its operational goals by concentrating on safety, hazard communication, and operator/maintenance skills.

Technical training at Carrier is located in the operations function. This placement gives training increased credibility and brings it closer to jobs and employees. Carrier trains approximately 30 percent of its total work force each year. The mainstay of its centralized training is a corporate training council. The council, which meets monthly, is composed of the president; division managers, including the training manager; and line managers. Because of the council structure, all training receives constant qualitative feedback from line managers, is routed through a centralized mechanism that determines needs and provides evaluative data on learning transfer based on division manager input, and directly supports operational strategies and goals because it is incorporated into the planning process. The training manager is privy to corporate change prior to implementation and can therefore develop training plans and courses to directly support operational goals.

Training Allocations

No discussion of the role of work-based learning and how it is structured in employer institutions would be complete without a look at how America's training is allocated.

Table 2 shows the distribution of formal employer-based training by sex, race, and ethnicity. Women receive a slightly disproportionately larger share relative to their share of employment. Whites receive a disproportionately larger share compared with blacks and Hispanics.

Most formal employer-based training — 68 percent — is provided to employees between the ages of twenty-five and forty (see Table 3).

How extensively formal employer-based training is used varies significantly by industry (see Table 4). Industries that use formal training the most are those with high concentrations of personnel who can benefit the most from such training — managers, professionals, technicians, and sales personnel. Regulation and certification requirements typical of industries such as mining and health care also encourage formal training.

**Table 2. Formal Training by Sex,
Race, and Ethnicity of Trainee (by Percentage).**

Demographic Group	Share of Training	Share of Work Force
Males	53.3	55.5
Females	46.6	44.4
Whites	92.2	86.0
Blacks	5.1	9.5
Hispanics	2.7	5.5

Source: U.S. Census Bureau, 1987.

Table 3. Formal Training by Age of Trainee (by Percentage).

Age	Share of Training
16-17	0.15
18-19	0.54
20-24	8.84
25-34	38.75
35-44	28.83
45-54	14.82
55-59	4.46
60-64	2.62
65 +	0.98

Source: U.S. Census Bureau, 1987.

Table 4. Formal Employer-Based Training by Industry, 1984.

Industry	Share of Total Training (Percent)	Training Intensity (Courses per Employee)
Agriculture	0.7	0.2
Mining	1.6	1.8
Construction	2.2	0.4
Manufacturing	18.7	0.9
Lumber	0.3	0.4
Furniture	0.2	0.3
Stone, clay, glass products	0.4	0.6
Primary metals	0.5	0.6
Fabricated metal products	0.9	0.7
Machinery, except electrical	4.2	1.7
Electrical machinery	3.2	1.5
Motor vehicles	1.4	1.3
Aircraft	0.8	1.4
Other transportation	0.9	0.4
Instruments, toys	1.0	0.9
Food	0.9	0.6
Tobacco	0.1	1.0
Hospital	10.9	2.7
Welfare, religious	2.8	1.3
Educational	10.8	1.4
Other professional	6.0	2.1
Forestry, fishery	0.2	1.5
Public administration	9.7	2.1

Source: Calculated from U.S. Census Bureau, 1987.

Small Versus Large Employers. Small employers (fewer than five hundred employees) account for roughly half of all jobs in the American economy and 40 percent of new jobs being created (Hamilton and Medoff, 1988). Small employers are important trainers because they create so many new jobs and because they tend to draw their employees from populations and industries that most need employer-based training. As Table 5 shows, employees in small businesses tend to be younger and less well educated than employees in larger businesses. Small businesses also tend to hire more Hispanic employees (but fewer black employees) than do larger employers. In addition, low-productivity service jobs tend to be concentrated in small business (see Table 6).

Table 5. Demographic Characteristics of Employees by Size of Employer (by Percentage of Employees).

Demographic Characteristic	Size of Employer (Number of Employees)			
	1–24	*25–99*	*100–499*	*500 +*
Age 16–24	30.3	25.7	23.2	22.7
Less than 12 years of education	22.7	22.1	20.5	17.8
Hispanic	5.8	6.5	5.1	5.0
Black	6.8	8.5	8.9	11.1

Source: U.S. Small Business Administration, 1988.

Table 6. Employment Jobs by Size of Employer (by Percentage of Employees).

Sector	Size of Employer (Number of Employees)			
	1–24	*25–99*	*100–499*	*500 +*
Service	79.1	69.5	61.6	58.2
Manufacturing	23.9	30.5	38.4	41.8

Source: U.S. Small Business Administration, 1988.

Small employers tend to operate in relatively small markets and, therefore, tend to have jobs characterized by broad
assignments of responsibility. Technologies also tend to be less
specialized than in larger businesses. The lack of specialization
makes both the employees and the employers flexible and provides a generalized learning experience that aids in career
transitions. However, small employers do not have enough
employees to afford the lost time from work required for training during working hours. As a result, employees in small
businesses tend to get less training than employees in larger
businesses, and the training they do receive tends to be more
concentrated in informal categories (see Table 7).

Persons who work for small employers tend to get their
training off the job. Data from the U.S. Small Business Administration show that in firms with fewer than a hundred employees,
three-quarters of employees who receive training are trained off
the job, compared with 58 percent of employees in larger firms
(U.S. Small Business Administration, 1988).

As demonstrated in Table 8, the relative importance of
employer-based training increases dramatically with the size of
the firm. Large employers tend to pay for more of the training
taken by their employees outside the workplace. Other data in-

Table 7. Average Hours Spent in Training
Activities in the First Three Months on Job,
by Size of Employer (by Percentage of Hours).

Activity	Size of Employer (Number of Employees)				
	1–49	50–99	100–499	500–2,000	2,000+
Formal training programs	11.8	8.8	10.3	29.2	22.1
Watching other workers do the job	45.0	50.3	45.1	55.4	69.5
Informal training by management	76.0	67.0	76.2	75.7	70.1
Informal training by co-workers	44.7	45.8	51.4	74.6	45.0

Source: Bishop, 1982.

dicate that employers with fewer than a hundred workers pay for 23 percent of the training taken outside the workplace, whereas employers with more than a hundred workers pay for 32 percent of the training taken outside the workplace.

Table 8. Sources of Job-Specific Training by
Size of Employer (by Percentage of Employees).

Source of Training	Size of Employer (Number of Employees)			
	1-24	25-99	100-499	500 +
Apprenticeship program	5.8	8.3	3.8	4.7
Business, commercial, or vocational school; junior or community college	32.9	25.6	28.3	23.2
Program at college or university	4.3	4.0	5.7	3.6
High school vocational program	9.4	6.3	6.5	5.0
Military	4.8	5.9	4.2	4.3
Previous or current employer	27.0	36.8	38.1	48.5
Other	15.7	13.1	13.4	10.7

Source: U.S. Small Business Administration, 1988.

Employer-provided training is a shadow education system that functions as a silent postscript to employees' formal schooling. It contributes to base learning, technical expertise, and the development of leaders for the nation's businesses.

Management of the training function, like most training itself, is driven by necessity. Economics, politics, regulatory requirements, and the competitive production cycle all influence how training will interrelate with the other functions of the organization.

A significant amount is expended on training by employers in all industries. Both large and small businesses conduct training, but the amount and type of training that people receive vary widely.

CHAPTER 3

Who Receives Training: Occupational Patterns and Needs

When one looks at the scope of job-related education and training in the United States, it becomes obvious that there is not enough of it. As shown in Table 9, only 55 percent of Americans have preparation for their jobs, and only 35 percent receive any upgrading once they are on the job.

The table also shows that human capital in the United States is unevenly distributed. Professionals are the most highly trained group, followed by technicians, management support specialists such as accounting managers and personnel managers, general managers, mechanics and repairers, precision production workers, and craft workers. In these occupational categories, 61 percent to 94 percent of employees get training to qualify for their jobs, and 26 percent to 63 percent are upgraded once they are on the job. Among clerical workers, sales employees, and extractive workers such as miners and oil workers, roughly half of employees get qualifying training, and a third receive upgrading. The least educated and least trained employees are machine operators, service workers, transportation workers, and laborers. In these categories, 18 percent to 37 percent of employees have qualifying training, and 14 percent to 25 percent receive upgrading.

Table 9 reveals other general characteristics of job-related training in the United States:

• Preparation to qualify for a job is more common than upgrading once on the job.

44

- Qualifying training more often involves formal education and informal learning on the job than it involves formal learning on the job. For upgrading, however, the three sources of training are usually of more nearly equal importance.
- Employer-based training — formal and informal combined — is a more important source of qualifying training and upgrading than is schooling. Moreover, employers pay for a substantial share of job-related education. Among Americans who used education to qualify for their jobs, about 8 percent had their courses paid for by employers, and employers paid for the courses of 41 percent of those who used education for upgrading.

Managerial Personnel

Executives. There are roughly 2.5 million executives and senior managers in the United States. They represent the top decision makers in a work force approaching 120 million people (Fullerton, 1987). Executives ride atop the managerial ladder, making policy decisions, shouldering overall profit-loss responsibility, and setting organizational objectives. The major difference between their current jobs as executives and their previous jobs as managers is that now they are required to make more decisions, in general, and more risky decisions with far-reaching consequences, in particular.

Executives must also have more contacts with groups outside the organization, including government agencies, other organizations, other countries, and the general public. When executives and other leaders set a new corporate direction, the executives must lead as well as manage.

By the time employees reach the executive ranks, they have already benefited from extensive human capital development. They have been trained for specific jobs as they moved through the managerial ranks. They have also received substantial developmental training — traditional schooling and training as well as job rotation and mentoring — that prepared them for "succession" to higher management.

Once executives break into the rank of upper manage-

Table 9. Sources of Qualifying and Upgrading Training: All Employees (by Percentage).

Occupational Group	Percentage with Qualifying Training				Percentage with Upgrading			
	Total	From School	Employer-Based Formal	Employer-Based Informal	Total	From School	Employer-Based Formal	Employer-Based Informal
All employees	55	29	10	26	35	12	11	14
Nontechnical professionals	92	87	6	16	47	47	10	11
Management support specialists	77	52	11	38	52	20	20	17
General managers	71	43	12	39	47	18	17	16
Clerical	57	33	7	31	32	10	10	15
Sales	43	15	12	28	32	7	13	15
Service	36	13	9	18	25	7	8	12
Transportation	36	2	8	26	18	2	6	9
Machine operators	37	6	6	26	22	3	4	16
Laborers	18	2	2	13	14	2	2	10

Technical workers, technical professionals	94	83	14	23	63	25	23	17
Technicians	85	58	14	32	52	20	18	19
Craft	66	11	16	44	26	7	7	13
Precision production	61	17	15	38	36	8	13	18
Mechanics and repairers	68	19	18	39	44	7	22	17
Extractive	56	4	13	48	34	6	13	18

Source: U.S. Bureau of Labor Statistics, 1985.

Note: Individual percentages can add up to more than the totals because some employees received training from more than one kind of source.

ment, they continue to receive an average of 36.3 hours of formal training per year (Lee, 1987). Participating in corporate task forces, on-the-job coaching, and mentoring provide executives with significant informal training in leadership roles as well.

About 70 percent of large U.S. companies have some ongoing effort for educating executives, even though executive education involves only about 0.75 percent of the total employee population (Fresina and Associates, 1986). Large, successful manufacturing firms have the most extensive and institutionalized executive development programs, while the banking and transportation industries seem to invest the least in executive training. A 1987 survey indicated that executive training absorbs 12 percent of the total training budget in *Fortune* 500 companies (Stephen, Mills, Paw, and Ralphs, 1988).

Executive training and development tend to be centrally managed and delivered by training professionals. Most employers, especially in manufacturing, routinely charge back all costs of executive education to the operational departments; however, in 40 percent of companies, the overall corporation pays. In 81 percent of large corporations, executive education is administered centrally, usually one or two levels below the chief executive officer. The executive education staff typically consists of one or two people who collect and broker program information and counsel the executives to be trained (Fresina and Associates, 1986).

At least two-thirds of companies that have executive education describe it as "individual development" or the building of leaders. Typical executive development programs focus on leadership, communication and motivation, and strategic planning.

Historically, the most common delivery method for executive training has been the seminar, usually provided by a university. Executive training has been unique in its reliance on sources outside the organization. Roughly half of all executive training involves special programs developed by universities, professional associations, and highly specialized consultant groups, either commercial or nonprofit. Anecdotal evidence, however, suggests a more recent trend toward executive development programs provided internally or bought outside but tailored to the individual employer's needs. The trend toward bringing executive development inside the employer institution reflects a felt need to provide a context specific to each employer's institutional culture and strategic niche as well as conducive to the development of the working team.

In general, the success of executive training is subjectively measured, in part because executive performance is rarely subject to formalized performance review. Where formal evaluation is conducted, the most common practice is for the executive or the executive's superior to evaluate the transfer of training to daily activities. In-house trainers (or consultants, who provide the training in many situations) are not routinely involved in following up on training.

Managers. There are more than five million managers in the United States (Fullerton, 1987). Managers are the fifth most highly trained occupational group in the American work force, after technical professionals, nontechnical professionals, technicians, and management support personnel (see Table 9). The pattern of training for managers is typical of that for most Americans. As shown in Table 10, most management training is provided at entry level. Formal education and informal training are the dominant sources of qualifying training, but for upgrading, managers rely on formal employer programs as much as on education and informal training.

Managers in financial jobs get more qualifying training from their employers than do other managers. Public managers and managers in medicine and health care get the most retraining from their employers. In general, public and private managers are about equally likely to receive formal and informal qualifying training, but more public managers than private managers get formal and informal upgrading.

Most working adults spend half their nonsleeping lives being directed by managers (Kotter, 1982). Unlike an executive, a manager executes policy rather than sets it. A manager frequently directs supervisors, generally has concrete data to work with when undertaking a task, and (among management staff)

Table 10. Sources of Qualifying and Upgrading Training: Managers (by Percentage).

Kind of Manager	Percentage with Qualifying Training				Percentage with Upgrading			
	Total	From School	Employer-Based		Total	From School	Employer-Based	
			Formal	Informal			Formal	Informal
All managers	71	43	12	39	47	18	17	16
Public	70	47	14	35	65	23	32	27
Private								
Financial	83	54	17	46	57	22	21	19
Personnel	76	41	7	39	55	15	23	17
Sales	74	44	21	46	52	16	24	21
Health	78	61	18	30	64	24	32	6

Source: U.S. Bureau of Labor Statistics, 1985.
Note: Individual percentages can add up to more than the totals because some employees received training from more than one kind of source.

often has the most frequent interaction with others in the organization. The manager is the "translator" who conveys policy and motivates the work force toward achieving corporate goals.

Senior managers in major corporations generally have a large number of people reporting to them through other managers; they have considerable influence with executives on policy decisions. Middle managers are responsible for fewer employees, direct workers with supervisory responsibilities, and influence policy through senior managers.

Manager training, particularly for middle managers, is common among American employers. Although new managers usually begin with a good educational base — college degrees are the rule rather than the exception — they often have little training in motivating and managing people. As managers move from their areas of technical expertise, taking on the responsibilities of coordinating resources and people, they need a wider array of skills. The traditional response of American employers, therefore, has been to "make" managers through extensive training, including on-the-job training and mentoring.

In large employer institutions, senior managers are responsible for the training and development of the managers who work for them. The delivery system for training most managers is therefore highly decentralized. Management development programs are often developed and controlled centrally, however. The professional training staff supports senior management by providing advice and creating and delivering programs for training and developing managers. Judgment of the superior(s) is the most common vehicle for determining training needs of individual senior managers or selecting more general development programs.

New managers are most often trained in employee selection, decision making, team building, strategic planning, and budgeting. Experienced managers receive developmental training in subject areas that will make them more effective in groups, institutions, and the external community. Developmental training includes subject matters such as interpersonal skills, negotiation, teamwork, organizational development, and leadership. Most large companies promote understanding of social and political issues through training seminars and conferences.

Middle managers are a prime target of formal corporate training activity. Training for middle managers has been the most uniformly applied training effort of American companies over the past decade. Approximately three-quarters (73.8 percent) of all private companies provide some formal training for their middle managers (Lee, 1987). In 1987, such training represented 22.4 percent of the *Fortune* 500 human resource development (HRD) budget—the largest share devoted to any occupational grouping (Stephen, Mills, Paw, and Ralphs, 1988). On average, each company that trains middle managers provides about thirty-seven hours of training a year to each of seventeen middle managers.

About half of American companies train senior managers. Each such company provides an average of ten senior managers with thirty-four hours of training a year (Lee, 1987). Employers also support both job-related and non-job-related courses for managers through tuition assistance programs.

As a manager's responsibility and salary increase, mentoring, job rotation, and outside seminars tend to replace formal in-house training. Training delivery for time-conscious managers is often through small groups and is sometimes deliberately held off site to avoid telephones and other distractions.

The in-house training staff is the most frequent provider in 65 percent of *Fortune* 500 companies, supplemented by outside consultants and coaching and mentoring (Stephen, Mills, Paw, and Ralphs, 1988). At the beginning and middle-manager levels, more companies rely exclusively on in-house sources than at the senior level. In contrast, at the senior level, more companies use outside vendors and consultants alone than at lower levels.

Smaller companies rely more on outside suppliers and informal methods than do larger companies. Large companies have enough resources to develop customized programs and enough managers to make the costs of developing and maintaining an in-house training department worthwhile.

Training for managers is evaluated more often than training for executives, but evaluation is still largely subjective. Large companies most often evaluate developmental programs using trainees' opinions (31 percent) and supervisors' opinions (29 percent). In the *Fortune* 500 companies alone, 54 percent of companies frequently use the superior's opinion to evaluate whether the training changed job performance, and 46 percent ask trainees (Stephen, Mills, Paw, and Ralphs, 1988).

Quantitative evaluations are rare. If there is a return on investment (ROI) evaluation, it is usually done at the conclusion of the program or course. Six-month follow-up evaluations are infrequent among the *Fortune* 500 companies.

Supervisors. The supervisory work force includes close to 5 million American employees. More than half of these are in retail sales occupations. Roughly 2 million more supervise blue-collar employees in American industry. Another 700,000 are supervisors in office settings. The remainder are scattered throughout the nation's industries (Fullerton, 1987).

As shown in Table 11, supervisory training follows a pattern similar to that for management training but at reduced levels. In general, supervisors are slightly less likely to get employer-based training than are managers. Supervisors tend to have substantially less formal education for job preparation or upgrading. With the exception of police, fire, and office supervisors, less than 20 percent of supervisors use job-related education to prepare for their jobs, and only 10 percent use formal education for upgrading.

In contrast to a manager, a first-line supervisor directs workers who make goods or perform services and who, as a general rule, do not supervise others. A supervisor implements new corporate directions at the point of production or service delivery and trains other workers, whether as an overt part of the job or through subtle behavioral cues that signal the supervisor's preferred methods of operation.

Almost no one moves directly into a supervisory position. Even if the new employee is academically well prepared for a management role, there is typically a period of two to three years on the job before the supervisory assignment. If a supervisor is new to the company, usually he or she has been a supervisor somewhere else. Often, skilled technical workers become super-

Table 11. Sources of Qualifying and Upgrading Training: Supervisors (by Percentage).

Supervisors by Occupational Group	Percentage with Qualifying Training				Percentage with Upgrading			
	Total	From School	Employer-Based		Total	From School	Employer-Based	
			Formal	Informal			Formal	Informal
Mechanics and repair persons	68	15	22	43	58	5	38	22
Police and fire	58	24	26	34	78	39	35	33
Extractive	56	7	14	55	34	12	20	21
Office	59	25	13	37	50	16	24	16
Craft	70	17	13	55	25	8	6	11
Production	56	16	12	39	44	12	18	19
Sales	50	18	11	34	34	7	13	14
Food preparation	53	13	11	33	31	9	5	19
Cleaning services	41	7	7	30	25	4	12	10
Agricultural	32	9	7	27	34	3	8	28

Source: U.S. Bureau of Labor Statistics, 1985.

Note: Individual percentages can add up to more than the totals because some employees received training from more than one kind of source.

visors, and strong technical skill is essential to maintaining the respect of production workers. However, new supervisors soon find that technical expertise is not enough and that a range of interpersonal and managerial skills is required to be a successful supervisor.

The content of the training for first-line supervisors reflects the employer's culture — including the extent to which employees are to be involved in decision making and the methods used to maintain a productive, informed, and satisfied work force. Most companies emphasize traditional management skills in training first-line supervisors. Employer-sponsored courses cover topics ranging from communications and leadership to company policies and how to conduct performance evaluations.

Technological changes have dramatically affected the first-line supervisor's job. Computerized information systems now allow top management to dip directly into the ranks for information. At the same time, new technologies and a greater reliance on working teams at the point of production and service delivery have made working teams more autonomous. The supervisor has had to assume a less aggressive role in managing work processes and a more supportive role in facilitating the work of front-line teams. In some industries, the demise of middle management's role as information organizer and gatekeeper has propelled first-line supervisors to assume new linkage and information-gathering roles. In some cases, hierarchical levels have collapsed: middle and first-line management have combined into teams that work on all aspects of operations with nonsupervisory personnel. This new participative management requires the first-line supervisor to spend more time dealing with conceptual and human resource issues than previously.

In 1987, about 59 percent of all the large private companies offered some formal training for first-line supervisors, and those that did provided an average of thirty-three hours per supervisor (Lee, 1987). *Fortune* 500 companies allocated about 22 percent of their HRD budgets to supervisor training in 1987 (Stephen, Mills, Paw, and Ralphs, 1988).

In-house training departments are the major agents of supervisor training. For example, 81 percent of *Fortune* 500 companies responding to a survey indicated that the in-house department is "always or frequently" used for supervisor training, and this training is the "primary charge" of the HRD department in 11 percent of these companies. Exclusive use of the in-house source is more common for supervisors (25 percent of companies with formal training) than for other levels of management personnel (17 percent and 10 percent for middle and senior management, respectively). Most companies (64 percent) use both inside and outside providers. Only 11 percent use vendors alone (Lee, 1987).

On-the-job coaching is almost universally available, and in companies that do not provide formal training for first-line supervisors, coaching may be the sole source of training. Overall, coaching is generally considered to be the most common delivery method, with the immediate superior as provider.

The supervisor's superior usually evaluates whether the skills targeted in training actually transfer to the workplace. Self-evaluation occurs in 40 percent of *Fortune* 500 companies, a slightly smaller percentage than for the middle and executive management levels. Evaluation by in-house trainers is almost as common as self-evaluation.

Management Support Specialists

Apart from technical professionals, nontechnical professionals, and technicians, management support specialists are the most highly trained employees in American employer institutions. There are more than three million employees who provide management support in staff functions such as accounting, underwriting, personnel, labor relations, and training (Fullerton, 1987). The training pattern for these workers tends to parallel the training pattern for managers (see Table 12). Qualifying training for support professionals tends to emphasize schooling and informal OJT. In general, there is less upgrading than initial training, even though there is more formal employer-based training for upgrading than for job preparation.

Table 12. Sources of Qualifying and Upgrading Training: Management Support Professionals (by Percentage).

| Management Support Professional | Percentage with Qualifying Training | | | | Percentage with Upgrading | | | |
| | Total | From School | Employer-Based | | Total | From School | Employer-Based | |
			Formal	Informal			Formal	Informal
All management support professionals	77	52	11	38	52	20	20	17
Financial	79	49	16	43	58	23	28	21
Human resources	74	38	11	43	60	18	26	23

Source: U.S. Bureau of Labor Statistics, 1985.
Note: Individual percentages can add up to more than the totals because some employees received training from more than one kind of source.

Nontechnical Professionals

There are close to 9 million nontechnical professionals in the United States, including roughly 5 million teachers, librarians, and counselors and more than 3.5 million other professional specialists, such as lawyers, artists, designers, writers, and photographers (Fullerton, 1987). Individuals in these occupations get more qualifying training than those in any other occupational group except technical professionals. They are unique in terms of the large amount of qualifying training and upgrading they receive from schools. In fact, no occupational group relies more on schooling for preparing for their jobs and upgrading after they are on the job than do teachers. Lawyers and teachers are the most highly educated and trained nontechnical professionals. Photographers and artists get substantially less education and training (see Table 13).

Nontechnical professionals are generally defined as degreed workers who have attained specialized expertise in a given area other than the physical or natural sciences or mathematics and who have their careers focused in their area of expertise. They are usually workers who are salaried but exempt from receiving overtime pay when their work week extends beyond forty hours, according to the U.S. Fair Labor Standards Act.

Nontechnical professionals can be found throughout modern companies, working as members of the management staff and in specialized support divisions — as patent and tax attorneys; writers and editors; personnel, labor relations, and training specialists; and librarians who perform information searches and maintain specialized corporate libraries.

Nontechnical professionals generally have a great deal of autonomy in their jobs and are expected to work with a minimum of direct supervision. They make decisions related to their own areas of expertise and create their own methods for achieving major goals, often in concert with technical professionals. They are also expected to be motivated and able to set and meet objectives that contribute to achieving the larger corporate goal.

Professionals often have considerable latitude in working hours — and frequently choose longer hours than required, per-

Table 13. Sources of Qualifying and Upgrading Training: Nontechnical Professionals (by Percentage).

Nontechnical Professional	Percentage with Qualifying Training				Percentage with Upgrading			
		From School	Employer-Based			From School	Employer-Based	
	Total		Formal	Informal	Total		Formal	Informal
All nontechnical professionals	92	87	6	16	47	47	10	11
Teacher	95	96	6	12	70	57	9	9
Librarian	78	68	2	26	53	30	9	9
Lawyer	95	92	3	17	55	15	9	10
Writer, editor	84	61	7	53	32	14	6	13
Photographer	81	41	13	42	48	19	6	20
Artist	83	67	5	33	32	20	1	7

Source: U.S. Bureau of Labor Statistics, 1985.

Note: Individual percentages can add up to more than the totals because some employees received training from more than one kind of source.

haps because of a strong work ethic, intellectual interest, or belief in the significance of a particular project to their profession.

Significant projects, special benefits, training, contact with respected peers, access to expensive facilities, and individual freedom are incentives for a nontechnical professional to continue in a job. Excessive management requirements, lack of recognition, and limited opportunities for learning are among the most frequent causes for departure. Quality of work life and potential for growth as well as increased income are important criteria in their employment decisions. Therefore, many corporations encourage professional growth through participation in professional societies, university teaching, or consulting. Corporations also create learning opportunities and other options — including high-salaried but nonmanagerial jobs — to retain professionals.

The main reasons that corporations invest in training for professionals are to maintain expertise (update professional knowledge), meet needs arising from new projects, orient professionals to corporate goals and culture, provide an incentive for hiring and retention, and help employees manage stress and improve their health.

There is little information available on the training courses provided specifically for professionals, probably because much of this training is technical (and is measured in that arena) or comes from the general corporate training curriculum available to all managerial, technical, sales, and professional employees (time management, stress management, writing, and the like). However, professionals and corporate training executives interviewed for this study cited the following topics as frequent focuses of training:

- Specialty skills (professionals frequently choose updating in their fields when training is elective)
- Computer literacy
- Time management and project scheduling
- Report writing and English (writing is a primary function of most professionals)
- Speaking and presentation skills

- Interpersonal skills such as negotiation techniques
- Health and stress management
- Orientation to the company's goals and strategies
- Opportunities for career and professional development
- Topics related to social concerns such as the company's equal employment opportunity policy and employee safety programs

According to the 1987 Lakewood survey, 48 percent of large corporations provide training for their professionals, who receive an annual average of thirty-six hours of training per person. Of companies providing professional training, 64 percent use a combination of in-house and outside sources, 27 percent use outside vendors only, and 10 percent use in-house providers only (Lee, 1987). According to interviews conducted for this book, evaluation of professional training is most often subjective, and ROI is rarely calculated.

Clerical Personnel

There are more than twenty million clerical personnel who provide administrative support in the United States. More than five million process financial records, and more than four million are secretaries. The remainder are clerks or dispatchers or have other information management functions (Fullerton, 1987). As shown in Table 9, a little more than half of clerical personnel have qualifying training and less than a third get upgrading. These workers fall in the middle range of American employees in terms of the proportion who have qualifying training and upgrading.

There is mounting evidence that a growing share of clerical employees are undertrained. Information-based technology is increasing the skill requirements and importance of clerical employees. The clerical worker of today usually operates a computer—over 82 percent of companies with more than 10,000 employees use computers for word processing (Lee, 1987). The average clerical worker has learned computer operation or a new word processing program within the past five years and now uses a personal computer for preparing letters, keeping records, and scheduling office events. Clerical personnel may also be responsible for training new clerical workers or even the professional staff on new office equipment.

Some clerical employees, such as executive secretaries, have the responsibilities of power and confidentiality. Such workers usually need top-quality clerical skills, good social skills, supervisory skills to manage other administrative support personnel, good appearance, and the ability to stay calm under pressure.

Clerical time saves management time. In many instances, clerical employees have assumed tasks previously done by managers and other specialists, and with computer power, clerical workers can do more in less time. They have time for more editing, processing, drafting, and accounting-type functions and can assume more administrative tasks; professionals and supervisors now delegate more of their duties to clerical personnel. This "skill migration" from managers, professionals, and other specialists is fueling debates on compensation and may push up wage scales.

Clerical positions are unique in their consistency from organization to organization; their core duties tend to be similar across all industries. These jobs are also unique in that they tend to have a limited career track that flows to executive assistant and then stops. To move up significantly in salary, the clerical worker has to acquire a different job title and shift tracks to an administrative or supervisory position such as office manager or purchasing director. Alternatively, she or he can change companies, leveraging skills into more pay.

Clerical worker turnover is high in prosperous regions, where the supply of qualified clerical workers tends to be small and companies compete for good clerical personnel. In recent years, the opening of other career paths to women has affected the availability of good clerical personnel. Because the clerical field is largely female dominated with a limited career path, it has suffered the loss of many people who would have seen it as a viable career option in the past.

In general, the investment in formal employer-provided training for clerical workers is low because they usually enter the work force with most of the basic skills (typing, shorthand, filing procedures) that enable them to do their job. High school vocational programs, community colleges, and trade and business schools usually provide this preparation. Increasingly, however, shortages in qualified clerical personnel are driving employers to create their own clerical workers rather than buy them. Also, clerical workers with strong basic clerical skills frequently need upskilling when computers are introduced into the office or a new word processor or information management software is brought on line. In fact, as employers have aggresssively invested in word processing and other computerized office technology, they have increasingly found that clerical workers are the key to its efficient use. Thus, clerical training courses include orientation to the employer's chosen software for word processing, mailing lists, information management, and other functions. Other clerical training courses include telephone communications, spelling, time management, business writing, language and interpersonal skills, and career development.

According to interviews conducted for this book, employers rarely or never conduct needs assessments for clerical training. Faced with a training challenge whenever new machinery is introduced into the office, many companies elect to send their clerical workers to outside courses, which are often provided by the equipment vendors. However, training needs are often more extensive than those addressed in the vendors' overviews because manuals designed to facilitate the integration of machinery are often complex. Consequently, more in-depth outside training, usually in the form of seminars, is needed. Frequently, however, even this opportunity is offered selectively — only one member of the clerical staff may go for training and, on returning, train fellow workers.

Fifty-three percent of all companies have formal secretarial-clerical training. The average company provided 26 clerical workers with 16.9 hours of formal training each in 1987 (Lee, 1987). Also in 1987, *Fortune* 500 companies spent roughly 6 percent of their training budgets on clerical training (Stephen, Mills, Paw, and Ralphs, 1988).

Interviews conducted for this book reveal that only about 10 percent of clerical training is formal. The in-house seminar is the most common format for formal training, but 35 percent of all companies now use some computer-based training, mainly to teach computer-related skills such as word processing and spreadsheeting (Lee, 1987).

Interviews also reveal that the usual practice is to use both in-house and outside providers for clerical training (44.5 percent of companies). Sole use of the in-house training staff is more common than sole use of outside vendors (36.5 percent versus 18.9 percent, respectively). Training purchased from vendors is often noncustomized, but 50 percent of companies that have clerical training use customized vendor training for clerical personnel (Lee, 1987). The prime responsibility for clerical training is usually at the corporate level, with major responsibility colocated at the plant, department, office, or store.

Evaluation of clerical training in technical skills is frequently experiential. The worker goes to training and is then expected to apply the skills on the job. Manpower, Inc. (a prime trainer of clerical personnel placed as temporary workers in offices), tests workers extensively, maintaining that "the only true method of testing lies in assessing an operator's ability to apply skills and knowledge to a realistic work sample" (Hamburg, 1985). To test for office automation skills, Manpower requires the trainee to create a document from handwritten draft through proofreading and final printed copy.

Training in the "softer" side of clerical work (including interpersonal skills and time management) is infrequently evaluated. When it is, evaluation is generally subjective, gauging the participant's reaction to the training.

Sales Personnel

There are almost thirteen million marketing and sales employees in the United States. Most are concentrated in retail sales. More than two million of the nation's sales workers are cashiers, another four million are retail sales workers, and another million are stock clerks. The remainder sell commodities, business services, real estate, securities, and insurance (Fullerton, 1987). Sales workers rely less on education than on employers for the training necessary to qualify for their jobs and to upgrade their skills once they are working (see Table 14). The extent of training varies substantially among sales representatives. Those who sell insurance, real estate, securities, business services, and commodities have substantially more job-related education and employer-based training than those who sell retail products and personal services.

The success of current business strategies and the development of innovations frequently hinge on the skills of the sales force. "Customer service" strategies are impossible unless the sales force is well trained in this arena. Innovation strategies depend heavily on the ability of sales employees to recognize customers' needs for new applications of existing products. Sales personnel also need to be carefully integrated into the culture and structure of the company if they are to communicate new applications and other innovations up the line. Sales personnel are in a unique position to feed such information back to product development departments, along with information on what the competition is offering. If the sales operation is in tune with the rest of the organization, it can be the company's "investigative" division.

Sales managers tend to agree that employers can develop successful salespersons with careful selection and training. According to a recent survey, the typical sales training manager thinks that the superstar's success stems 48 percent from attitude, 25 percent from selling skills, 13 percent from product knowledge, 11 percent from experience (the previous sales record), and 4 percent from work effort and good assignments (Fresina and Associates, 1988). Attitude, selling skills, and product knowledge can be learned through training on the job. Careful selection is also important. The skills and knowledge that a salesperson brings to the job should generally fit the industry, company, product, or group of customers. For example, a salesperson who sells technical products or services requires a technical background; a person selling financial services requires a financial background.

Sales training focuses on new product orientation, product updates, attitudes and interpersonal sales skills, negotiation,

Table 14. Sources of Qualifying and Upgrading Training: Sales Workers (by Percentage).

Sales Worker	Percentage with Qualifying Training				Percentage with Upgrading			
	Total	From School	Employer-Based		Total	From School	Employer-Based	
			Formal	Informal			Formal	Informal
All sales workers	43	15	12	28	32	7	13	15
Finance and business services	75	34	33	35	58	17	27	19
Commodities	55	24	12	38	40	9	21	17
Retail and personal services	27	5	5	20	20	3	5	13

Source: U.S. Bureau of Labor Statistics, 1985.
Note: Individual percentages can add up to more than the totals because some employees received training from more than one kind of source.

and procedures (paperwork). Common courses include general selling skills, presentation skills, business writing, telephone skills, customer service, account management, planning, time management, goal setting, problem solving, stress management, and technical training specific to a product or industry (Fresina and Associates, 1988).

Data from two recent surveys indicate that product knowledge and selling skills are two of the most common focuses of corporate sales training (Honeycutt, Harris, and Castleberry, 1987). But at least one study has shown that investment in selling skills can have a huge payoff: improving sales technique alone provided returns of as much as 1,660 percent (Fresina and Associates, 1988).

Sales training accounts for roughly 16 percent of the training budget in *Fortune* 500 companies (Stephen, Mills, Paw, and Ralphs, 1988). Virtually all companies train new hires, and more than half of large companies have formal policy statements outlining the number of sales training hours required, the courses to be taken, and the deadlines for completion. A company usually provides at least 48 to 80 hours of initial sales training, with some companies requiring 160 hours or more. Established salespersons receive about 43 hours of training per year (Lee, 1987). About 16 percent of employer-based professional development for salespeople is through formal training; about 75 percent is through coaching by the sales manager (Fresina and Associates, 1988).

Training provided by in-house sources is the most productive type of training, according to sales training managers and vice-presidents responding to a 1987 survey (Fresina and Associates, 1988). However, such training does not necessarily involve the in-house training department. A wide variety of people and organizations, ranging from the in-house training department to sales managers to outside consultants and universities and colleges, provide sales training. In fact, in most *Fortune* 500 companies, sales training is usually provided by someone other than the in-house training department.

Sales training managers, vice-presidents of sales, and, to a somewhat lesser extent, chief executive officers are responsible for tying the goals for professional development of the sales force to the corporate goals. Objective training goals (for example, trainee increases number of calls made by 5 percent within the next six months) are used by 84 to 90 percent of companies. Training managers or sales managers usually assist designated trainers in setting training goals, with salespersons involved in only 28 percent of companies (Fresina and Associates, 1988).

Lectures are still the most common delivery method for sales training, and less than 50 percent of training programs for salespeople are "canned" (standardized, meaning that the same program is delivered regardless of company, industry, product, or kind of customer) (Fresina and Associates, 1988). Canned programs tend to cover generic sales skills, whereas more tailored training programs focus on product knowledge and other company-specific subject matters.

Videotaped presentation is popular because of its flexibility. It enables training immediately after hiring, introduces new products without bringing all salespersons to one location, and demonstrates products consistently to everyone. Custom video is expensive but cost-effective compared with using untrained salespersons in the field. Videotaping the salesperson in action is also useful for showing how he or she comes across to customers; videotaped role play is increasingly becoming a standard tactic in sales training (Fresina and Associates, 1988).

The most common means of evaluating sales training courses is soliciting the trainee's opinions, or the "smile test." Sales training is more carefully evaluated than management training, in part because the sales process is more easily quantified. Tests for learning retention are administered less than 35 percent of the time, and less than 25 percent of companies use cost-benefit analysis; about 50 percent of companies use customer evaluation as an indicator of a salesperson's performance and thus an indirect indicator of training's effectiveness (Fresina and Associates, 1988).

Customer Service Personnel

As the nation's service sector grows, so grows the importance of high-quality customer service. Many kinds of workers share the challenge of providing high-quality customer service, but none are more directly involved than the direct customer service workers. They are the link between the company, the product, and the consumer. Advertising may make promises, but customer service workers must deliver.

Although business willingly acknowledges the important role of the customer service worker, compensation has not kept pace with praise. Many workers are in low-pay categories, have minimal (if any) benefits, or work only part time. Entry-level positions and minimum wages are common.

The "baby bust" of the 1960s and 1970s may affect customer service jobs more than other jobs. The demographic forces of the 1970s were the cause of so many service enterprises whose profitability depended on minimizing wages, training costs, and capital investment. This trend could be reversed in the 1980s and 1990s. The worker shortage has already become a major problem in the fast-food industry (Zemky and Meyerson, 1985). Of the 3.5 million people who work in this industry, 70 percent are age twenty or less. Workers in the fast-food industry are usually first-time employees, and the job serves as a transition between home and school (Charner and Fraser, 1986b). In retail, the employees are mainly part-timers, and the problem is turnover. According to Alice McCord of the National Retailers Association, "The industry faces a young, poor-quality applicant" (Kimmerling, 1986).

Customer service training, therefore, will become increasingly important. One survey noted it as second in importance only to management training in projections for 1988 and beyond (Bureau of National Affairs Staff, 1988). Interviews conducted for this book reveal that customer service training usually involves courses in interpersonal skills and customer relations. Because so many customer service workers are first-time employees, they need basic orientation to workplace customs. Also, much of their training comes under the general rubric of sales training. Customer service training courses cover topics such as product and service orientation, problem solving, negotiation, selling, customer interaction skills, stress management, basic clerical skills, and computer keyboarding.

Despite its growing importance, there are few available

data on customer service training per se. The 39.6 percent of employers that train their customer service personnel provide about 26.8 hours of training annually per person. Overall, 5.86 million customer service workers were trained in 1987, for a total of 157 million hours of training (Lee, 1987).

Only 13.3 percent of companies that provide formal training rely on outside sources alone; 42.7 percent use a combination of in-house staff and outside providers, and 44 percent provide formal training using in-house staff only (Lee, 1987). Prime responsibility for training customer service workers rests at the divisional, group, or subsidiary level.

Companies conduct very little evaluation of customer service training. However, in many cases supervisors observe the interactions of employees with customers and make subjective evaluations of the training's effectiveness. In some cases, such as telephone sales, phone calls to customers may be monitored and used by supervisors as an evaluation tool.

Service Employees

There are eighteen million service employees in the United States — seven million in food preparation, three million in building services, and roughly two million each in health, personal, household, and police and fire services (Fullerton, 1987). Overall, service employees are among the least educated and least trained American workers because of the low rates of education and training among food service workers and cleaning personnel. Health service employees, police and fire employees, and people in personal service occupations, such as barbers and child care workers, get much more training (see Table 15).

Technical Workers

Technical workers use theoretical principles from the mathematical or natural sciences in their work. They also tend to utilize substantial amounts of technical machinery or processes in their work and to work in industries that produce technical machinery or other products derived from the applica-

Table 15. Sources of Qualifying and Upgrading Training: Service Workers (by Percentage).

Service Workers	Percentage with Qualifying Training				Percentage with Upgrading Training			
	Total	From School	Employer-Based		Total	From School	Employer-Based	
			Formal	Informal			Formal	Informal
All service workers	36	13	9	18	25	7	8	12
Police and fire	56	18	29	24	55	20	28	21
Health	62	29	15	27	42	9	11	22
Building	14	3	2	10	24	9	12	20
Personal	52	34	12	12	29	9	8	6
Food	24	2	3	20	15	2	2	11

Source: U.S. Bureau of Labor Statistics, 1985.

Note: Individual percentages can add up to more than the totals because some employees received training from more than one kind of source.

tion of mathematical or scientific theory. Technical workers are especially important to American competitiveness because they tend to work in industries that produce the lion's share of internationally traded products and services. Technical workers are also important because they invent and produce the technologies that result in the upskilling of all workers. Ultimately, the continual integration of new technologies with more highly skilled labor is the engine of American competitiveness.

Attempts to define technical training and the technical work force are always somewhat arbitrary. The definition used here — that technical employees use theoretical principles from mathematics or the natural sciences in their work — is no exception. In general, this definition includes technical professionals (for example, scientists, doctors, and engineers), technicians, and technologists concentrated in both manufacturing and health care; craft workers concentrated in the construction trades; and skilled workers concentrated in manufacturing. By this definition there were 20.3 million technical workers in the United States in 1986, amounting to 18.2 percent of the American work force (Fullerton, 1987).

Table 17 shows that of all occupational groups, technical professionals, who number almost 4.8 million (24 percent of the technical work force), get the most education and training in preparing for their jobs and also get the most upgrading. The nation's 3.7 million technicians, who make up 18 percent of the technical work force, get more education and training in preparation for their jobs and more upgrading once they are on the job than any occupational group except technical and nontechnical professionals. There are almost 11.8 million blue-collar technical workers (58 percent of the technical work force), including precision production workers, mechanics and repairers, extractive workers, and craft workers (Fullerton, 1987). Blue-collar technical workers get only slightly more preemployment education and training and upgrading than the average American worker. Moreover, they rely much more on informal learning on the job than do other technical workers.

The nation's almost seven million machine operators and assembly workers are not included in the figures just given even though the jobs of these workers are increasingly technical in content. As discussed earlier, automated manufacturing is increasing the depth and range of skills required in the jobs of machine operators and assembly workers, and many are being consolidated and upgraded into technical jobs. Although they are difficult to count, it is clear that many operators and assembly workers have already become technical workers, including as many as two million who work in high-tech industries.

As shown in Table 9, operators and assemblers get relatively little preparation for work or training once they are on the job.

Although the workers in some technical occupations, especially in health care, are predominantly women, men dominate the technical work force, totaling 76 percent of all technical workers. As shown in Table 16, women, blacks, and Hispanics are generally underrepresented in the technical work force.

Technical workers are distributed unevenly throughout the economy. About 1.5 million are self-employed, principally as doctors, engineers, carpenters, mechanics, and repair workers. The largest number of technical workers is found in the service sector, mostly in health care. Manufacturing employs about 14 percent of all technical workers.

From another point of view, technical workers are most concentrated in the construction industry, in which one-third of all workers are technical workers. Mining, transportation, and utilities are next, with nearly one-fifth of their employees in technical occupations. In manufacturing, services, and government, about one worker in six is a technical worker.

Table 16. Percentage of Women, Blacks,
and Hispanics in Technical Occupations, 1986.

Occupational Group	Women	Blacks	Hispanics
All workers	44.4	9.9	6.6
Technical workers	24.3	6.4	4.8

Source: Adapted from Fullerton, 1987.

Technical workers earn well above the average for all workers (see Table 17). Male technical workers earn more than their female colleagues, but the disparity is less in technical occupations than in the economy as a whole. In technical occupations, female workers earn 84 percent of what male workers earn; in the economy as a whole, female workers earn 69 percent of what male workers earn.

Table 17. Median Weekly Earnings by Sex, 1986 (in Dollars).

Occupational Group	Both Sexes	Men	Women	Ratio
All workers	358	419	290	.69
Technical workers	482	501	420	.84

Source: Adapted from Fullerton, 1987.

Technical Professionals. Technical professionals are educated and trained to make broad judgments, to invent, and to apply a particular intellectual discipline to problem solving. In health care, technical professionals include employees responsible for making diagnoses and prescribing treatment to be provided by others. In other industries, technical professionals are responsible for developing new products and designs, enhancing existing products, and conducting research but are not necessarily responsible for formal management or exercising direct authority over subordinates. Technical professionals are most critical in the overall design and development phase of the competitive cycle and the diagnostic phase in the provision of health care services.

Technical professionals include the nation's 2.5 million health professionals, 1.5 million engineers, and 800,000 natural, mathematical, biological, and computer scientists.

Technical professionals' jobs most frequently require at least a four-year college degree and often require formal schooling beyond the undergraduate level. As shown in Table 17, technical professionals are the most highly educated and highly trained of the nation's employees. Relative to other employees, they tend to receive substantial amounts of both education and employer-provided training—formal and informal—both to qualify for their jobs and to upgrade skills once they are on the job.

All technical professionals rely heavily on schools to prepare them for their jobs. However, relative to other technical professionals, engineers and mathematical and computer scientists rely less on schools and more on employers for qualifying training (see Table 18). This suggests that engineering, mathematical, and computer jobs are more tailored to a particular employer and the employer's product, resulting in less carryover of academic training into the workplace.

Health professionals get the most upgrading of all technical professionals and rely more on schools than on their employers for both qualifying and upgrading training, suggesting that skill needs are not employer specific and that health care professionals have a stronger bond with their profession than with specific employers.

Technical professionals usually receive training in subject matter that applies broadly to a specific area of expertise. Because of the breadth of potential application, in the past organizations have played a relatively passive role in training their technical professionals, most often providing only general guidance and funding. However, in recent years the pressures of competitiveness have encouraged companies to integrate the development and design of innovations with production and marketing. The attempt to build more integrated R&D structures has encouraged more institutional control over the training and development of technical professionals.

Technical professionals, however, are still relatively autonomous in their professional development. Although most of their training is intended to update skills or knowledge in the face of new technology, the exact application of these skills and knowledge is usually left to the individual. For example, a seminar might introduce a new synthetic material and explain its development, properties, and uses. The design engineer who will use the material in new products will use the information much differently than the engineer who will test the products once they are developed.

Table 18. Sources of Qualifying and Upgrading Training: Technical Professionals (by Percentage).

Technical Professionals	Percentage with Qualifying Training				Percentage with Upgrading			
	Total	From School	Employer-Based Formal	Employer-Based Informal	Total	From School	Employer-Based Formal	Employer-Based Informal
All technical professionals	94	83	14	23	63	25	23	17
Architect	94	91	13	31	41	10	7	23
Engineer	90	73	14	33	57	23	28	18
Health	96	96	10	7	72	33	8	8
Mathematical and computer scientists	90	66	26	41	65	21	36	24
Natural scientists	97	91	9	26	59	30	25	15

Source: U.S. Bureau of Labor Statistics, 1985.
Note: Individual percentages can add up to more than the totals because some employees received training from more than one kind of source.

The technical professional's ability to glean diverse applications from generic material makes seminars and symposiums, such as those offered by colleges and universities, professional organizations, and other public providers, a good alternative to in-house training curricula. In 1987, companies in all sectors spent approximately $117 million to send their technical professionals to seminars. Colleges and universities are the most frequent source of outside seminars, drawing $41.1 million per year in revenues to train technical professionals from private industry.

Vendors are another major source of training for technical professionals. Vendors supplied approximately $175 million worth of off-the-shelf training materials, custom materials, and other training support services to technical professionals in 1987. Other sources of training (both in house and outside) for technical professionals account for an additional $1.4 billion per year.

A growing number of manufacturing companies are presenting training in integrated manufacturing to their technical professionals. Integrated manufacturing covers all phases of manufacturing from concept development through design and development to producing the finished project. The root principle of the integrated manufacturing perspective is to bring elite technical professionals together with production workers, sales and marketing personnel, and other members of the institutional team. The ultimate purpose is to reduce the cycle time required to integrate new technologies and to get innovations to market, to improve efficiencies and quality, and to encourage new applications. In addition, with such training, technical professionals can be responsible for more than one job or process rather than a single function or process, as was previously the case. This technique parallels the technique of cross-training, which is becoming increasingly common among technicians and craft workers and is resulting in a more knowledgeable and more versatile work force that is more responsive to organizational, technological, or industrial shifts.

Technicians. There are approximately 3.7 million technicians in the United States — more than 1.5 million health technicians; almost 1.3 million technicians in engineering and the sciences; and another 800,000 broadcast, computer, and air traffic technicians. Next to professionals, technicians are the most highly educated and well trained employees in the American work force (see Table 9, page 47).

A technician is an employee whose primary expertise lies in a particular specialty area. Although technicians have considerable depth of knowledge and highly developed skills in their specific areas of expertise, they lack the breadth of knowledge in the theoretical aspects of their specialties that is required of technical professionals. And although many technicians are graduates of four-year colleges, many have developed their skills and knowledge at technical or vocational schools or community colleges or, on occasion, through on-the-job training.

Many workers in the health care field, including nurses, physical therapists, x-ray technicians, and other operators of diagnostic equipment, are good examples of service-sector technicians. Technicians from manufacturing include circuit board assemblers and quality control technicians who oversee laser equipment in automobile assembly plants.

Technicians usually receive training that applies directly to their jobs. The training has its basis in theory but is focused more directly on the application of theory to the job than is training for technical professionals. Because technician training has a mixed focus of theory and application, a mix of instructional methods is necessary to ensure adequate skill acquisition and transfer. Most technician training includes three phases of instruction:

1. Introduction of the theories or principles behind the technology
2. Demonstration of the application of the theories, principles, and processes in a job environment
3. Hands-on practice of the skills and knowledge application in a simulated work setting

Like training for technical professionals, technician training includes generic courses. Unlike much training for technical professionals, however, most technician training is sequential and job specific and includes principles of new technologies (primarily equipment and processing techniques) and new applications for existing technologies. Technicians also take special courses required for licensing or certification, or "refresher" courses required for license renewal or recertification. Virtually all technician training is directed toward upgrading or updating skills.

Because of the hands-on nature of the technician's work, courses in safety and hazards are required. Technicians also receive specific training in procedures required for successful job operation, especially if the procedures are mandated by a government agency. For example, technicians in a drug company receive training in clean room operation and maintenance, laboratory technicians in a hospital receive training in maintaining sterile equipment and recording patients' test results properly, and technicians in a nuclear power facility receive training in emergency shutdown and evacuation procedures.

Of the more than $3.28 billion spent by employers each year for outside training and training support services, approximately $103.2 million is for technician training. Because of the nature of technician training, programs sponsored by colleges (including two-year colleges), universities, or professional associations are a frequent source of training outside the organization itself. Of the $68.9 million provided technicians each year to attend outside seminars and conferences, university-sponsored programs account for $24.1 million. Vendors, especially "original equipment manufacturers" (OEM), also supply a considerable amount of technician training and related support materials.

The amount of time technicians spend in training varies widely according to the job held, the company's support for training, and state and local certification (or licensing) requirements. There are few data available concerning the length of training specifically for technicians.

Blue-Collar Technical Employees. The nation's blue-collar workers number almost thirty million craft workers and operations personnel: construction workers, repair persons, precision production workers, extractive workers, machine operators, assembly workers, transportation workers, and laborers (Fuller- ton, 1987). According to the definition used here, only the preci- sion production, craft, and extractive workers; mechanics and repairers; some of the machine operators; and some assembly workers are technical workers. The remainder of the blue-collar work force is the labor pool from which new technical workers evolve.

With the exception of extractive workers and machine operators, roughly two-thirds of blue-collar technical workers get some kind of formal or informal preparation for their jobs, substantially less than the proportion of workers who get quali- fying training in the white-collar and technical professional populations (see Table 9). Blue-collar technical workers tend to rely on informal training on the job more than do workers in other occupations for the qualifying training and upgrading they get.

Equipment manufacturers are a vital source of training when the training goal is skill update. The rationale behind OEM training is that the manufacturer has a better understand- ing of equipment, processes, and procedures than any other source and is, therefore, most qualified to conduct training. Many companies that use OEM training purchase it as a part of the acquisition cost of new equipment. Unfortunately, no funding figures are currently available for OEM training.

When recertification or relicensing is the training goal, corporate training strategy often specifies two tracks, high-tech and low-tech. Craft and operations workers in high-tech jobs are likely to attend training sponsored by local colleges, voca- tional-technical schools, or professional groups. (This is espe- cially true for jobs requiring a specific number of hours of training or continuing education units for recertification or certification at a higher level of proficiency.) Employees in low-tech opera- tions jobs are more likely to receive their recertification train- ing through in-house programs, which are provided locally to minimize time lost from the job and to allow for tailoring to fit local needs.

A number of different sources can provide cross-training and retraining, depending on the specific kind of training needed.

Training by the equipment manufacturer is appropriate if operation, maintenance, or repair of new or complex equipment is involved. Local colleges or vocational-technical schools are good providers when training must cover basic principles and will involve laboratories or when the company would incur a great expense for equipment that would be used only in training. Much cross-training also takes place, formally or informally, on the job.

Data-Processing Personnel. The growing importance of data processing has created a distinctive population for training. Although individual categories of workers might seem more rightly to belong in other occupational categories, the industry that they serve (data processing) makes it more appropriate to treat them as a separate cohesive occupational group.

There are more than 1.5 million data-processing personnel in the United States, including information managers. This encompasses more than 300,000 computer systems analysts (computer scientists are also in this category), almost 500,000 programmers, more than 300,000 operators, and roughly 400,000 data entry clerks; the rest are information managers (Fullerton, 1987). Systems analysts (including computer scientists) are technical professionals, and information managers are in the category of managers. Programmers fall somewhere between professionals and technicians, depending on their responsibilities. Operators and data entry clerks use the computer as a job aid and neither create nor manipulate technology. Since they do not use theory in their work, they cannot be considered technical workers, according to the definition used in this discussion; they would probably normally fall into the category of clerical personnel.

Data-processing personnel are among the most highly educated and highly trained occupational groups in the American work force. As Table 19 shows, both systems analysts and programmers receive about as much education and training to qualify for their jobs as persons in any of the major occupational categories, and operators and data entry personnel get more qualifying training than persons in all but a few of the occupational categories. The proportion of systems analysts and programmers who get upgraded compares with the figure for technical professionals, the most intensively upgraded group, and computer operators get about as much upgrading training as general managers. Data entry personnel, however, get much less upgrading than qualifying training.

Systems analysts get substantial schooling, usually in colleges or universities, to prepare for their jobs, but they rely on formal and informal employer-based training for upgrading. For the most part, programmers use a combination of schooling from colleges and junior colleges, employer-based formal training, and informal OJT both to qualify for their jobs and to upgrade their skills on the job. Operators use a similar mix of schooling and training on the job.

With the exception of data entry clerks, data-processing personnel get more formal and informal employer-provided upgrading than persons in any of the major occupational groupings.

Data-processing personnel are a product of the information age. They build information systems and programs. They operate computers, compile and structure data, and input data into computers. Their primary product — information — may be sold to external sources or may be used internally as the raw material of institutional efficiency.

The structure of data-processing operations in an employer institution is similar to the structure of most technical functions. Systems analysts and computer scientists perform research, development, and design functions outside the line structure of the institution. Information managers are in charge of daily operations and the work of programmers and operators. In many cases, a substantial number of operators and data entry clerks are in departments outside of computer departments, creating a highly decentralized network of customers for the data-processing operation.

With the downsizing of computer hardware through the miniaturization of circuitry and the spread of user-friendly technology, data-processing operations are becoming ever more dispersed. As a result, data-processing personnel are serving multiple roles in R&D centers and line departments and serving as service and training providers for the rest of the institu-

Table 19. Sources of Qualifying and Upgrading Training: Data-Processing Workers (by Percentage).

Data-Processing Worker	Percentage with Qualifying Training				Percentage with Upgrading Training			
		From School	Employer-Based			From School	Employer-Based	
	Total		Formal	Informal	Total		Formal	Informal
Computer systems analyst	94	70	27	45	64	16	37	25
Computer programmer	91	64	19	41	61	25	27	24
Operator	74	34	15	43	45	13	17	26
Data entry clerk	71	31	14	41	27	5	8	14

Source: U.S. Bureau of Labor Statistics, 1985.

Note: Individual percentages can add up to more than the totals because some employees received training from more than one kind of source.

tion. In order to cope with dispersion, some employers have established a new staff department, the information center, which is an intermediary between data-base managers and end users. The center is charged with providing training, applications, and support to the computerized departments throughout a given company. Even with user-friendly programs, communicating with the computer means learning a foreign language. Information centers perform a coordination and training function, helping end users produce spreadsheets and graphs and integrating applications and hardware between departments.

Advances in information-based technology have been the major source of changing skill requirements in most American jobs. Data-processing occupations continue to be hardest hit by the whirlwind of changing skill requirements that emanate from the ever new information technologies. This fact explains why data-processing employees receive so much qualifying training and upgrading. It also explains why so much of their training is employer provided. The technology is simply moving too fast for employers to wait for schools to catch up.

Ironically, computer programs sometimes replace their creators. Jobs that originate with new technology are eventually simplified. For example, general-solution business applications such as Visicalc and Lotus 1-2-3 are reducing the demand for computer programmers. Moreover, it is no longer necessary for programmers to understand hardware architecture or to design separate data structures for each application—two skills that distinguish a programmer analyst from a mere programmer.

Interviews conducted for this book indicate that, with the exception of data entry clerks, data-processing personnel generally have college degrees or have attended structured programs at technical schools and received certification. Frequently, courses include managing information systems, computer design and analysis, auditing (of both systems and procedures, including security measures), and programming in specific computer languages such as BASIC, FORTRAN, and COBOL.

Armed with basic education or certification, the aspiring data-processing worker usually enters the work force as a development specialist or a beginning programmer. Hands-on experience and on-the-job training are then the keys to professional development.

Expertise in a particular kind of information system is gained through experience and is essential to career mobility. Data-processing personnel often market themselves to employers on the basis of knowledge of a particular system and its programming requirements. From the employer's perspective, information managers who already know the essential elements of the employer's computer system can adjust rapidly to their new jobs. Hiring experienced people is simply the most cost-effective approach to hiring what is usually high-priced technical talent.

Information systems are highly tailored to the specific structures and products of employer institutions, encouraging formalized training for new data-processing personnel to ensure speed, consistency, and quality of learning. The most common delivery method for formal training is the seminar. Information managers spend an estimated hundred or more hours per year in formal computer-related training.

The rapidly changing technology of the computer field drives data-processing personnel to keep their knowledge current by reading trade journals, attending conferences, interacting with vendors, and networking with colleagues through professional societies. User groups of data-processing personnel who use the same technology are a regular tool for problem solving and training. Information managers who manage other computer professionals, as well as computer systems, reported in interviews conducted for this book that although a college degree may be essential for movement into management in this field, support and mentoring from supervisors are often the most important ingredients for success on the job. This fact accounts for the relatively high level of informal on-the-job training among data-processing personnel.

PART 2

Partnerships to Meet Training Needs

CHAPTER 4

Learning Partnerships: How Employers Form Linkages with Training Providers

Changing demographics and rapid technological advancements place a premium on workers who can adjust to and develop in today's workplace. Providing training for those workers is a big job, and employers frequently find that they cannot handle it alone. Therefore, over the years, linkages between businesses and training providers such as educational institutions, unions, public job-training underwriters, and private training vendors have become increasingly important.

Linkages, for the purpose of this chapter, are relationships between employers and providers that exist for the purpose of providing job-specific training to a targeted group of employees.

Providers are constantly marketing their products to potential clients; employers are bombarded daily with phone calls and mail encouraging them to buy particular products. However, employer training purchases are rarely made on the basis of slick brochures or friendly phone calls from a provider. Employers view the information they gather through these channels as tools to assist them in their selection, but generally linkages that result in an employer's purchasing a training product or program are originated by the employer. The reason for this is clear — training linkages are based on employer need; that is, an outside provider is called on when an employer requires help in responding to its training needs.

The person within the employer institution who actually makes the contact with the provider varies among employers and by circumstance. When an employer institution has a centralized training function, staff in that department are the most likely to contact providers. When training is decentralized, the contact person may be housed in an operational department or at a plant site. Contacts with providers may be made from any level within the employer organization — company training director, operational manager, line supervisor, training staffer — depending on who has the authority to explore and ultimately sign off on the training purchase.

Forming Linkages:
A Common Business Transaction

Corporate training practitioners claim that forming a linkage is a common business transaction: the decision to go outside is much like any other business purchase. This belief holds true regardless of the frequency with which any given company may use an outsider provider. In most cases, establishing linkages is as simple as picking up the phone and contacting a desirable provider. For example, an employer identifies a problem, believes it can be resolved through a training program, and seeks to fulfill the training need within the unique constraints of her or his organization. If the need cannot be met with in-house resources, a decision is made to purchase training. A search is then conducted for a provider who can meet the training need. The distinguishing characteristic for linkages, therefore, is not in *how* they are formed but rather with *whom* and for *what reasons*.

Employers generally enter into a questioning process before they invest in outside training. Questions vary first and foremost by the type of training required (managerial, clerical, and so on) and second by the characteristics of an employer's specific needs within each stage of the training process. For example, questions generated from a training needs analysis are unique to both training area and employer environment. These questions aid in the search for a provider and ideally surface before the search for a provider begins.

Other variables may also influence decisions regarding which providers are used, how they are used, and their level of involvement in developing and delivering training programs. These variables include:

- Type of industry and unique needs it might have
- Size of the company, especially the training department, and size of the training budget
- Types and levels of the people being trained
- Personal contacts the trainer or employer might have with outside providers
- Geographical proximity of the provider
- Local economic conditions, such as availability of prepared personnel and training needs of the local population
- Government incentives to conduct training or to buy training from specific providers

Training linkages do not necessarily mean contracting with a provider from start to finish. An employer rarely picks up the phone and orders a complete training program. A provider might offer a comprehensive service, but employers often do not need or cannot afford the whole package. Most commonly, employers use a combination of inside and outside resources; a balanced mix of these resources enhances training programs by providing the best of what is available.

Examining the Make-or-Buy Decision

The make-or-buy decision—the decision to build a program with in-house staff and resources or to purchase assistance from outside training experts—may be made for all or any part of a training program. The employer decision to make or buy is influenced by need, in-house capability, and available funding. The role of the provider is driven by those circumstances and thus can come in many shapes and sizes.

The make-or-buy decision usually hinges on how providers measure up to the needs and standards of the employer. The consideration and application of these standards are sometimes self-consciously systematic. Frequently, however, the purchaser considers what the provider has to offer in a more intuitive way and reaches the "buy" decision on instinct based on past experience.

Ideally, as one training practitioner noted, the desire to provide the best quality training product should be the primary catalyst driving the make-or-buy decision. But quality is not always the deciding factor. For example, an employer with some in-house training capabilities needs to develop a highly technical training program. A reputable vendor, well known for his expertise with this kind of program, is available. But cost consideration drives the employer toward attempting to develop the program with existing staff. Conversely, if cost is not an issue but time and convenience are, an employer may purchase a training program even though there is in-house expertise among the training staff.

The following criteria affecting the make-or-buy decision are cited most frequently by practitioners.

Expertise: The decision to make or buy based on expertise is most dependent on how specialized or unique the desired training need is. Specialized topics require greater expertise; more generic topics require less. Employers generally turn to in-house resources if the expertise exists. If in-house expertise is lacking, employers often seek an outside provider either to fill the need directly or to train individuals who become trainers. However, this criterion is not set in stone. If an organization has the expertise to conduct its training in house, it may look to outside sources for services or materials that will complement its resources. For example, a company may buy generic, readily available training materials such as workbooks, computer training programs, and video programs to offset costs of in-house development. Off-the-shelf word processing programs and sales or marketing workbooks are two products commonly "bought" by employers.

Employers usually rely on in-house expertise for employer- and product-specific training—training unique to a particular employer or product. Such training is governed by employer philosophies and procedures and is, therefore, not readily available in the external market. Given these boundaries, outside providers usually operate in an advisory capacity, assisting in-house experts with design and delivery.

Figure 1 shows the relationship between the specifications of the training need and the tendency to use an outside provider.

Figure 1. When Do Employers Seek Outside Expertise?

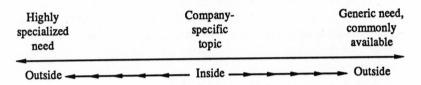

Highly specialized need	Company-specific topic	Generic need, commonly available

Outside ←————————— Inside —————————→ Outside

Timeliness: The make-or-buy decision is based on the time constraints surrounding training. If the in-house staff does not have the time to develop and deliver the program within the time frame requested, employers often seek outside services.

Size of population to be trained: The make-or-buy decision is based on the size of the training audience. The larger the training population, the more likely employers are to rely on in-house resources. The major impetus behind this decision is economics. For example, if there is a large "common need" for training, the likelihood increases that the program will be delivered more than once, thus resulting in economies of scale. However, when training is needed for only a few people, it is difficult to justify the time required for in-house development and delivery. Under such circumstances the decision to go with an outside provider becomes more practical.

Sensitivity or proprietary nature of subject matter: If the subject area of the training is sensitive or proprietary, the training is likely to be done inside regardless of other factors affecting the make-or-buy decision. Sensitive or proprietary training is defined as training used to gain a competitive advantage or training that gives access to proprietary, product, or strategic knowledge. Employers rarely issue security clearances to outside resources to provide training of this nature.

Cost considerations: Although cost is an important factor governing the make-or-buy decision, it is often considered in concert with other criteria. The economic outlays for training are only now coming to the forefront of the human resource arena. Cost alone has never been the reason to provide training, let alone to develop or deliver it in house versus outside. Sometimes it is more cost-effective to contract out, sometimes not. Therefore, most employers consider cost to be a secondary factor when deciding whether to make or to buy.

Employer conditions: The size of an organization or its training department affects the weight employers place on criteria affecting the make-or-buy decision. It is important to note that just because a company is large, it does not necessarily follow that its training department is large. A small employer or a small training department is less likely to have the expertise, resources, or time to meet a specialized need. A large department, in contrast, is more likely to have the resources necessary to conduct programs in house.

Other factors: An employer's decision to "buy" is not governed exclusively by the aforementioned criteria. An employer may use an outside provider to bring in new ideas or "new blood." Outside providers can rejuvenate a dull or boring training program that may then motivate employees to attend and learn. The make-or-buy decision can often be a moot point; a company may have a policy not to use outside resources because top management believes that the company should be able to meet all training needs with inside resources. Rarely, though, are there companies that *never* use outside providers.

Table 20 summarizes the above factors.

What Can Employers Purchase from Providers?

Employers must consider the extensive range of provider services before they can make informed purchases. As discussed earlier, an employer may elect to contract with a provider for an entire training program. It is just as common, however, for an employer to choose to work with an outside provider on parts of, rather than the whole, picture. A provider may be chosen to assist with a needs analysis only, or the employer — confident of the need and training focus — may select a provider to design

Table 20. Factors Affecting Make-or-Buy Decisions.

When to Stay Inside	When to Go Outside
Company has expertise	No in-house expertise exists
Need is company specific	Highly specialized or generic need exists
Time is available	No time is available
Large audience needs training	Small audience needs training
Subject matter is proprietary	Subject matter is not sensitive
Cost of going outside is prohibitive	Cost of going outside is beneficial

and deliver the training. In addition, the employer may decide to build institutional capacity for the future and to have an outside provider conduct "train-the-trainer" instruction for in-house staff who in turn will train other employees. For example, providers can do any one or a combination of the following:

- Provide assistance with the initial training needs analysis
- Provide expertise and guidance to assist in-house staff members with the design and development of an in-house program
- Design and develop a company-specific program that will be delivered by someone else
- Provide supplemental training materials (such as workbooks, software, audiovisuals, and so on) for an in-house program
- Deliver a program that was designed and developed elsewhere
- Train in-house trainers so that they are able to deliver a program in house
- Take responsibility for an entire program from analysis to delivery

Employers rarely "buy" customized comprehensive training packages from outside providers because such packages are expensive. Most commonly, employers look to providers for training materials. Other common situations include employers' linking with providers for actual delivery training or for training in-house personnel (training the trainer). Train-the-trainer linkages are growing in popularity because they are viewed as cost-effective. The employer pays for training one employee, that employee is then qualified to deliver training in house, and the employer has limited his or her outside training expenses.

One issue that surfaces when an employer decides which services to buy from a provider is whether to purchase a customized or an off-the-shelf program. A customized program is developed from scratch to suit individual needs. Customizing is costly and therefore limiting. An off-the-shelf program, sometimes called "prepackaged" or "canned," is by its very nature generic, providing general information within a particular subject area. Often prepackaged programs come with training for in-house staff who will eventually deliver the training. Training practitioners sometimes seek out canned programs because it is not always necessary to "reinvent the wheel." For example, an employer may choose a prepackaged computer training program because it does not need to be company specific, and it is less expensive and time-consuming than developing one in house. Employers and providers claim that 90 percent of training is based on off-the-shelf products and only 10 percent on customized programs.

Employers may also use a combination approach by purchasing a prepackaged program and then tailoring it to meet specific training needs. The general rule of thumb for this approach is to find a program that meets 80 to 90 percent of a company's training needs and to then modify it as needed. According to training practitioners, most off-the-shelf programs are subtly and gradually tailored to incorporate company-specific examples.

Whatever the provider role, a constant exchange of information flows between employers and providers. Table 21 illustrates the information flow according to the roles that the provider might play.

Identifying Providers

Locating a provider is much simpler when the employers have thoroughly examined their training needs. However, how

Table 21. Information Flow Between Employers and Providers.

Role of the Provider	Role of In-House Staff
Training needs analysis	Staff collaborates with provider to collect data necessary to conduct analysis
Consult and provide guidance for development of in-house program	Staff collaborates with provider to learn how to develop successful training program
Design company-specific program	Staff collaborates with provider to supply information on program content and to convey desired results
Develop company-specific program	Staff collaborates with provider to supply information on program content and to convey desired results
Provide training materials • Customized	Staff collaborates with provider to give information on what needs are
• Off the shelf	Minimal interaction between employer and provider—staff simply requests program on specific topic
Deliver training	Staff collaborates either significantly or minimally with provider, depending on training program or subject area needs
Train-the-trainer	Staff collaborates either significantly or minimally with provider, depending on who conducts training and whether it is conducted on or off employer site
Provide entire program from start (analysis) to finish (evaluation) • Customized	Staff collaborates with provider to supply data and information on what needs are and what employees should learn
• Off-the-shelf	Staff has little or no interaction with provider—a program is selected and provider supplies it—staff gives very little in way of specifications

employers go about identifying providers depends on their experiences and informal communication networks in the training
community. Employers with longtime dealings in human resource development almost always identify providers through
informal training networks specific to their training area or industry. These employers choose providers based on referrals
from peers and information passed on through professional
associations or trade shows. Very often, these employers select
providers who have been former employees or longtime colleagues. Providers discovered through these methods tend to
be local.

Formal networks are available to assist employers who
lack informal networks to locate the best providers. Some sources
of information are:

- TRAINET, a computer data base available to members of
  the American Society for Training and Development that
  contains information on a variety of training programs and
  providers
- *Bricker's International Directory,* a resource manual on executive
  and upper-level management programs at numerous colleges, universities, and independent institutes
- Directories published by professional or trade associations
  listing providers by subject area. Two publications available
  at public libraries are *Consultants and Consulting Organizations
  Directory* and *Training and Development Organizations Directory,*
  published by Gale Research Company.

Special Role of the Request for Proposal. A request for
proposal (RFP) is a formal, orderly, and systematic process
employers use to locate a provider who can offer the best product at the best price. Specifically, an RFP is a request written
by an employer asking providers to submit proposals stating
how and at what cost they could meet the employer's needs and
specifications. Governmental entities are required to use the RFP
process and to issue a public notice of their intention to secure
bids along with a time frame for receiving proposals. Once proposals are received, the employer begins a review process to select
the provider that most closely matches the employer's need at

the most affordable price. The RFP process can take anywhere from three to six months or longer. In many cases, it is much easier to select a provider in a less formal manner and to develop a training program in a much shorter time frame.

Overall, RFPs are not used very extensively, possibly because the time frame for securing bids often exceeds the time frame of the desired training program. Often, however, they are a required part of a business transaction such as those with the government. When RFPs are not required, they are most commonly used for very large or expensive projects.

Criteria Employers Use
to Distinguish Between Providers

A large number of providers exist, and many have similar products to sell. Employers must define criteria to serve as a framework in distinguishing among providers. Criteria commonly identified by employers are:

- Cost: Does the provider offer a desirable product at a reasonable cost?
- Credentials: Does the provider have any special certification or documentation that validates his expertise in a particular training area?
- Background: How long has the provider been in business? How long has the provider been involved with a particular subject area?
- Experience: Who (employers) has the provider worked with, and how successful was the relationship? What do the provider's references report?
- Philosophy: What beliefs and values does the provider hold? Does the provider prefer a particular approach to any given topic such as a particular management theory?
- Delivery method: What teaching methods does the provider use? Many employers are concerned with a provider's knowledge of and ability to apply adult learning theory. Also, what materials are used, and in what form are they presented (lectures, workbooks, audiovisuals, interactive videos)?
- Content: What topics will the provider cover in the program?

- Actual product: What will the actual program look like? Most employers want to see a sample presentation or will request that the provider develop and test a pilot program before a formal contract is made.
- Results: What can the employer expect as an outcome of the training?
- Support: How much support will the provider offer to the employer during the implementation of the program and follow-up?
- Request for proposal: How closely has the provider matched an RFP?

Armed with broad criteria and results from a needs analysis, employers move to the next level by developing specific criteria unique to each training area. For example, if the needs analysis shows that clerical workers are deficient in office etiquette, it is logical that a provider will be chosen based on her or his ability to supply those skills. However, one employer may believe that the most important criterion for such a provider is that she or he have a background that includes several years of work experience in an office setting. Another employer needing the same kind of training may believe that it is more important that the provider have a background that includes several years of teaching experience in the subject area and may not be as concerned with firsthand personal practical experience. Both employers are concerned with "background" criteria. However, they might select different providers because they are concerned with different aspects of the background criteria.

CHAPTER 5

Partnerships in Action

Vendors and Consultants

Vendors and consultants come in all forms. Some are large national, international, or local firms that offer a wide variety of training capabilities in almost all areas of training; others are small and specialized. Regardless of the size of a firm, the most common use of vendors and consultants is for training professional employees. Professional employees are defined as those whose jobs require at least four years of postsecondary education plus some additional education. (See Chapter Three for more information on professional employees.)

Vendors and consultants are the most extensively used providers because their sole purpose is to provide training for employers. They are, therefore, market driven. Employers select these providers because they have proven to be the most responsive to employer needs. They offer convenience, flexibility, and timeliness when delivering specialized services. For example, vendors and consultants are extremely mobile; they usually will come to the employer site regardless of where that employer is located. Vendors are also very flexible in scheduling and in the types of programs that they will do.

Employers most frequently solicit small firms of just one or two persons. This phenomenon most likely is because small firms outnumber larger firms. Individual entrepreneurs continue to enter the consulting market because it poses relatively few entrance barriers. Setting up a small consulting firm does not require a large staff, and equipment and overhead costs are low; anyone with expertise in a given area and a computer can set up shop.

Large consulting firms usually attract employers involved in large, expensive training projects. These employers find large consulting firms responsive to their time and resource requirements; money is not an issue. Large consulting firms usually have access to a wide array of prepackaged programs that can be easily tailored to employer needs as well as an available trainer "pool" ready on short notice to supplement in-house efforts. For employers who choose large consulting firms over small ones, it is like going to a large grocery store instead of the corner market.

A Snapshot: Steelcase and Learning International. Steelcase is a $1.7-billion international office products company manufacturing chairs, open-office furniture, and filing systems. The Steelcase network, headquartered in Grand Rapids, Michigan, consists of 500 authorized dealers. It employs 17,000 workers worldwide; approximately 400 members of its work force are sales representatives.

Steelcase primarily uses outside training providers to develop and deliver process-oriented programs that give their employees common, general skills. Steelcase believes that large consulting firms can meet this criterion better than can small ones. According to Steelcase, small consulting firms are a better choice for one-shot programs or event-oriented courses that train employees to react to specific circumstances.

In 1984 Steelcase determined a need for uniformity in sales training for its dealerships and began exploring options for providing such training. Several sales managers and dealerships recommended the use of Learning International, a firm that had provided Professional Selling Skills sales training for Steelcase employees in ten Steelcase dealerships.

Learning International, a subsidiary of the $3.2-billion Times Mirror Company since 1985, is one of the largest consulting firms in the world. Learning International employs 439 people in 36 locations worldwide. Although the company will not reveal its net worth, it claims to have greater revenues than any other vendor in the same category. The company's clients include many *Fortune* 500 companies.

Learning International provides training to all levels of employees primarily in the areas of sales, management, and customer service. In addition to offering packaged programs, Learning International creates entirely customized programs to meet special client needs. Learning International will also work with clients to incorporate company-specific role-play exercises into an existing program or will combine two or more programs to create a unique training solution that best meets the client's needs.

Learning International conducts most of its training at the client's location or at a site selected by the client. Learning International is frequently responsible for delivering its own training programs; however, the company also offers train-the-trainer programs.

The Professional Selling Skills program provided to Steelcase dealerships is the most popular sales training program in the world; to date, three million people have completed this program. Steelcase dealerships told corporate headquarters that the program, which was offered nationwide, was easy to administer. The dealers also reported that trainees retained the course information and used their newly gained skills on the job. In addition, Steelcase corporate headquarters contacted Learning International to work in concert with their in-house sales training efforts for corporate sales employees.

Steelcase contracted with Learning International for sales training materials and a train-the-trainer course for approximately eight Steelcase employees. Those eight Steelcase employees ("master trainers") then trained twenty others, giving the company fifteen in-house corporate sales trainers and thirteen in-house field trainers to deliver sales training. Steelcase also requested that Learning International serve in an advisory capacity for their in-house efforts to design customized training programs that corresponded with new product launches.

Since 1984, the Steelcase–Learning International partnership has brought training to three thousand employees. According to Steelcase, this linkage has facilitated better communication and understanding throughout the company because employees use the same sales approach and terminology. Moreover, Learning International provides support to Steelcase as needed. Because of the success of this linkage, Steelcase and Learning International continue to work together; Learning International provides train-the-trainer courses and presents new training programs at Steelcase's quarterly training specialist meetings (Marcia Heath, telephone interview, July 1988; Carol Gold, telephone interview, January 1988; Robert G. Schaeffer, telephone interview, October 1988).

Educational Institutions

The primary mission of educational institutions is to provide a broad, general education to students before they enter the work force. Employers most frequently use educational institutions to supplement employers' efforts. Despite their past role, today's educational institutions have enormous potential to meet the needs of employers because they are the creators and caretakers of knowledge and research. It is ironic that while the potential exists for great collaboration between education and business, in many cases true active collaboration is not taking place (Foster, 1986).

Several schools, however, have made progressive strides toward fulfilling employer-based training needs; they have established institutional entities that specifically address the needs of employers. For example, Maricopa Community College in Phoenix, Arizona, created a Services Division to coordinate employer training efforts. The Corporate Services Division acts as a broker between employers and educational departments for the nine community college campuses that constitute the Maricopa Community College system. The division offers a variety of services including standardized and customized training.

These progressive institutions are blazing the trail for other educational facilities. They are clearly demonstrating that educational institutions benefit from training partnerships with business. First, when faculty work directly with employers, they must remain up to date on the current applications of new techniques and innovations. Not only does this create a better pool of qualified teachers; it also serves to elevate the credibility of the institution in the eyes of the community and the nation. Second, linkages expose potential students to the educational institution. An employee participating in a training program conducted by a university may select that institution for further education down the road. If this happens, the educational institution realizes increased enrollments, which translate into greater revenues. In addition, partnerships with business help educational institutions gain access to placement opportunities for their traditional graduates. Finally, linkages with business may lead to grants and equipment donations from employers.

On the flip side, employers participating in linkages with educational institutions also have begun to recognize the benefits. First, educational institutions are relatively permanent and can offer continued services. Second, employees who attend training conducted by an educational institution often earn academic credit or continuing education units (CEUs) toward accreditation. No other provider can offer this benefit. Finally, educational institutions blanket the nation and are extremely accessible; almost all employers are within thirty minutes or less of some kind of educational institution.

Both employers and educational institutions have a lot to offer and gain from each other, but barriers do exist. Most of these barriers stem from the fact that the nature and mission of educational institutions are so different from those of business. Sometimes it seems as though neither understands the culture or operating structure of the other. However, as the two groups begin to work together, barriers will break down, culminating in success stories for each side.

Four-Year Colleges and Universities

The United States supports 156 universities and 1,853 colleges with a combined enrollment of almost 8 million students. These institutions spend almost $80 billion annually, or roughly

$13,000 per student. Colleges and universities provide more qualifying and upgrading training for American workers than all other postsecondary educational institutions combined.

Four-year colleges and universities are just beginning to recognize their training roles and to capitalize on potential opportunities for providing customized training. Several universities support independent management or executive development institutes. These institutes offer specialized "open" management courses for high-level employees. Employers usually contact the institute to register their employees; class attendance is not limited to one specific employer.

When universities do link with employers to provide customized training, it is not usually in technical areas. However, many institutions are a widely used source for continuing education. Most universities have not moved to create special offices that work specifically on customized training programs within industry. Usually these programs are coordinated by an employee in a continuing education department or another university office.

A Snapshot: General Tire, Inc., and Kent State University. General Tire, Inc., a $1.2-billion tire-manufacturing company, employs 12,000 workers in its North American locations. In 1987 General Tire, which is headquartered in Akron, Ohio, became a wholly owned subsidiary of Continental AG of Hannover (herein referred to as Continental), West Germany.

General Tire conducts most of its training in house using its ten-member training staff. Training programs focus on management development, quality improvement, and sales. General Tire uses outside resources to supplement in-house design and development efforts; outside providers are primarily used to supply materials and deliver programs. For example, General Tire regularly schedules sales training for its employees and contracts with an outside provider for video and self-paced sales training materials.

Following its acquisition by Continental, General Tire identified several employees who would have regular contact with the Continental office in Germany. These employees, ranging from support staff to engineers, needed to speak German to communicate by telephone or in their travels to West Germany. General Tire determined that these employees needed language training to fulfill these new responsibilities. Language training is highly specialized, and General Tire did not have the in-house expertise to provide such training. The company decided to seek an outside provider through an RFP process. Kent State University responded with an RFP describing how they would design and deliver language training.

Kent State University is a four-year public university located in Kent, Ohio. University enrollment is approximately twenty thousand students.

Kent State's College of Continuing Studies has provided customized training services to employers in the Akron area for approximately ten to fifteen years. Employer-based training is supported by the university's mission and is one part of its efforts to provide continuing education to nontraditional student populations. Moreover, employees completing company-sponsored training at Kent State are more likely to individually enroll in advanced courses at the university.

All employer-funded training at Kent State is coordinated by its College of Continuing Studies. The college employs two staff members responsible for developing and coordinating comprehensive customized training services, including identifying instructors from all academic departments within the university.

Most employer-supported training programs are geared toward middle management and supervisors. Topics include marketing, finance, effective business writing, and motivation.

Kent State uses a variety of methods — direct mail advertising, media advertising discussion forums, and word of mouth — to inform businesses of its training services. In addition, Kent State works to build and sustain relationships with local employers by asking business people to sit on advisory boards that help develop university curricula.

Kent State has a track record of providing management development training to General Tire employees, and General Tire is a regular participant at the Kent State Training Forum — a meeting designed to help university executives understand the training needs of area businesses. In January 1988 General Tire contracted with Kent State University for language training.

Through this linkage, Kent State University faculty trained fifteen General Tire employees in conversational German. Employees primarily involved in travel to Germany and identified for training by General Tire ranged from support staff to managers and engineers. The three-month training program required participants to meet twice a week (Carol Sesnowitz, telephone interview, September 1988; Robert Fish, telephone interview, December 1988).

Community Colleges and Junior Colleges

There are currently twelve hundred community colleges in the United States and its territories, and the majority are located within thirty minutes of most individuals. These two-year institutions serve the needs of a local population and are therefore considered to be particularly responsive to business, industry, and community needs. In fact, of all the educational institutions, community and junior colleges have taken the most aggressive, directed, and often progressive approach toward customized training. Most of these institutions support a special office for employer-customized training. Forty percent of all community colleges have campus-based business/industry/labor councils (BICs) that coordinate activity between the academic and business sectors to facilitate employer-based customized training. Seventy-five percent of all community colleges provide some customized training for businesses. Most employer training is geared toward technical and vocational fields.

A Snapshot: Gerry Baby Products and Front Range Community College. Gerry Baby Products is a $70-million baby product–manufacturing company. The company operates a plant in Thornton, Colorado, and employs approximately 360 workers. In 1987 Gerry expanded its product lines to include children's car seats, playpens, and high chairs. To keep production levels up during expansion, Gerry Baby Products planned to hire an additional hundred workers. At the same time, Gerry also formed a new partnership with the Takata Company in Japan to supply parts for the expanding product lines.

Gerry Baby Products was now faced with several training needs. First, current employees needed training on assembly and production techniques for the new product lines. Second, new hires needed training on current and new assembly and production techniques and an orientation to the company. Finally, all employees needed to overcome language barriers arising from the labeling of Japanese-supplied parts.

Gerry Baby Products does not have an in-house training department and frequently relies on outside providers. Most company training is limited to informal orientation programs and selected skills programs such as word processing. However, in 1987, when the president of Gerry Baby Products and a state board member governing Front Range Community College—a community college serving Gerry's geographical region and a formidable provider of employer-based training—met on an airline flight, the company embarked on a new, formal, and comprehensive training approach.

Front Range Community College (Front Range) is an innovative two-year college located in Westminster, Colorado. Founded in 1968, the college serves five counties; student enrollment on the main campus is over six thousand. In the fall of 1986, Front Range established an Office of Contract Training Services and Continuing Education to better meet the growing training demands from area employers. Prior to establishing this office, Front Range primarily offered prepackaged professional development courses such as communication skills, basic management, and supervisory skills for area employees. The office expanded Front Range's services to include customized training and a small business development center. The small business center, funded by the U.S. Small Business Administration, has assisted approximately two hundred companies in less than a two-year period.

Front Range has also been instrumental in moving Colorado communities toward partnerships with Japan. Working from an economic development approach, Front Range first established a partnership with a sister two-year college, Takayama College, in Japan, resulting in student exchange programs. In addition, Front Range gained access to Japanese businesses with international interests and helped to bring those businesses to Colorado. For example, Front Range was instrumental in initiating contacts between Japanese steel companies, Colorado officials, and businessmen. When relocations were successful, Front Range would negotiate contracts for providing employer-based training. Finally, with Front Range's efforts, Colorado opened an international trade office in Japan.

Gerry's training needs and Front Range's training services and international experience coincided to an overwhelming degree. In 1987, Gerry Baby Products contracted with Front Range for a comprehensive package that would integrate the three new product lines into Gerry's entire operation. A large part of this package involved the design and delivery of a comprehensive training program for new and existing line workers affected by the product line expansion. In addition, Front Range was responsible for developing training materials that would transcend language barriers and for securing additional training funds from the state "Colorado FIRST!" program — a program that offers training funds to new and expanding businesses.

In order to develop the program and materials, Front Range's instructional designers went to work on Gerry's assembly line and talked with employees. Through these discussions, Front Range put together an on-the-job training program, a video orientation program for new hires, and color-coded pictorial job aids for all line workers. The job aids illustrated the assembly line process and were packaged in loose-leaf notebooks so that they could be reorganized and changed to reflect changes in the production line. Most information was presented by pictures; words were kept to a minimum because many Gerry line workers spoke limited English. Colorful icons were used to highlight procedures that demonstrated safety precautions, quality issues, or special techniques for performing a task.

Both training and materials were crafted to integrate a management and inventory method that would be new for the entire Gerry operation. The method, called "just in time," provides a company with the ability to respond rapidly to change and requires workers to be extremely flexible and versatile. It relies on producing materials to fill customer orders on an "as-needed" basis, or "just in time," rather than producing ahead of orders and stockpiling products. For example, as Gerry received new orders, workers were moved to the assembly line as needed to fill those orders. Job tasks changed depending on the number of workers on the line, and job aids were changed to reflect that. The same technique was applied to inventory.

Gerry Baby Products and Front Range both benefited from this partnership. Gerry was able to successfully integrate three new product lines into their operation. In addition, when Gerry Baby Products made a presentation of the training procedures to its partner, Takata, some of the job aids were translated into Japanese. These translations helped demonstrate a willingness to understand the new culture and to strengthen the partnership. Front Range received an award from the National Society for Performance and Instruction for the job aids and training materials it developed for Gerry. Gerry Baby Products and Front Range plan to work together again in the near future. Gerry is planning to bring in four new product lines and has contacted Front Range for services, including training (Cary Israel, telephone interview, August 1988).

Secondary Schools

The nation's secondary schools provide occupational education to about 5.5 million students at a cost of about $6.5 billion per year. Secondary schools are not common providers of training to employers because the focus of these schools is not on the adult population. However, some have expanded their mission beyond the secondary level to address the needs of adults, especially those employed by local industries. Secondary schools and consortia of secondary schools or school districts are the primary providers of adult basic education programs that focus heavily on remedial or basic skills. Secondary schools deliver employer-based training outside of this realm only infrequently.

A Snapshot: Economy Linen and Licking County Joint Vocational School. Economy Linen and Towel Service of Zanesille, Inc. (herein referred to as Economy Linen), a wholly owned, independent subsidiary of the $2.5-million Economy Linen and Towel Services, Inc., is a commercial laundry company primarily serving the health care industry. Economy Linen's parent company was founded in 1931 and operates two plants, one in Zanesville, Ohio, and the other in Dayton, Ohio. The Zanesville plant was built in 1982.

By 1987 the Zanesville plant, which employs eighty-seven workers, had increased its business from three million to eight million pounds of laundry annually. As business increased, more manpower was needed, and this ultimately resulted in the promotion of seven production line workers to line supervisor positions. At the same time, the Zanesville plant employees moved to establish a union. Economy Linen brought in a management consultant team to review the concerns and demands of employees seeking to unionize. During ensuing negotiations, the employer sought training for all employees, especially those promoted from line to supervisory positions. After reviewing recommendations from the management consultant team, Economy Linen agreed to formal supervisory training to provide the new line supervisors with the necessary interpersonal and managerial skills to do their jobs. In addition, Zanesville plant employees became unionized.

Economy Linen had never offered formal supervisory training and made the decision to look for an outside provider with supervisory training expertise who could provide on-site, customized training. At that time, the company received a brochure from the Licking County Vocational Resource Center that outlined the services for which Economy Linen was looking.

Licking County Joint Vocational School (JVS) is one of fifty Ohio vocational schools charged with training adults as well as junior and senior high school students in vocational skills. The vocational school has provided customized training to area businesses for over ten years. Because of the growing demand for employer-based training, the school built a large Vocational Resource Center. The center offers comprehensive employer training services ranging from needs analysis to evaluation. In addition, it helps employers assess their employment and training needs when making decisions on hiring new or dislocated workers. The center's training services are extremely flexible and are geared toward employer needs: training is conducted at the employer site, in the center, or by satellite (teleconferencing); programs are customized and offered around the clock.

In 1987–88 the JVS provided 126 training courses to area employers. Programs ranged from technical training courses such as tool safety, blueprint reading, welding, pipe fitting, and meter repair to supervision and management training such as principles of banking and word processing.

In December 1987 Economy Linen contracted with Licking County Vocational Resource Center for a comprehensive supervisory training program. After determining Economy Linen's specific training needs through consultations with management, Licking County Vocational Resource Center designed and delivered a tailored supervisory training program for Economy Linen's seven new supervisors. Training included basic management techniques, communication skills, problem solving, and decision making. Classroom training was held at a location near the Zanesville plant; classes met for three hours every other week for four months. In order to maintain production at the Zanesville plant during training, Economy Linen brought supervisors over from its Dayton plant.

Both Economy Linen and Licking County Vocational Center recognized success from this cooperative effort. At Economy Linen employees gained new skills, production levels continued on the upswing, and employee morale rose. Licking County Vocational Center met the training needs of its client and secured another supervisory training contract from Economy Linen for 1989 (Ronald Cassidy, telephone interview, July 1988; George Dube, telephone interview, November 1988).

Vocational-Technical Schools

Vocational-technical schools, which include public and private postsecondary schools, are noted for marketing their programs to adult learners. In fact, these schools provide training to prepare over one million technical workers for jobs. Students at these institutions tend to be older, poorer, and in greater need of basic skills training than are students at four-year colleges. Vocational-technical schools are especially attractive to employed adults (a large percentage of the full- and part-time student body at these institutions is employed while attending classes) because of their accessibility and flexible class scheduling. Private schools in this category, in particular, are noted for their short occupationally related programs and their flexible scheduling.

The role of vocational-technical schools in providing customized employer training is very similar to the role of community colleges. Also, not surprisingly, vocational-technical schools specialize in customizing *technical* training for local employers. Some offer skills training and clerical training.

A Snapshot: Fred Jones Manufacturing Company and Francis Tuttle Vocational Technical School. Fred Jones Manufacturing Company (herein referred to as Fred Jones) of Oklahoma City, Oklahoma, is an authorized Ford Motor Company supplier of remanufactured engines and transmission and auto parts. This medium-sized company operates seven sales districts in seven states across the country and remanufactures approximately one million component parts annually.

Fred Jones must comply with stringent quality specifications outlined by its customers. Purchasers such as Ford Motor Company and General Motors regularly conduct quality assessment surveys of the suppliers. If quality does not meet customers' specifications, future and even current contracts may be jeopardized.

Fred Jones has long recognized that employee performance has a direct impact on quality. Because training is essential to increasing employee knowledge and skill about production techniques, Fred Jones has determined that more and better training is needed to help the company maintain its competitive edge.

For years, Fred Jones has relied almost exclusively on outside resources to create training opportunities for its employees. Fred Jones regularly contracts with outside providers — including local consulting firms and vocational schools — for customized training and participates in training programs offered by industry associations and equipment manufacturers.

In 1987 a General Motors (GM) quality assessment survey determined that Fred Jones needed to implement statistical process control (SPC) and gauge control systems to continue receiving contracts from GM. Fred Jones Manufacturing Company turned for training assistance to an organization that it had worked with in the past — Francis Tuttle Vocational Technical School.

Francis Tuttle is part of the Oklahoma vocational education system. The state is divided into twenty-eight vocational districts that promote technical and vocational training for area residents and businesses. Each district maintains a high-technology facility designed to support the needs of area employers. Most employers are well aware of Oklahoma's strong vocational education system before or as they enter the state because Oklahoma uses its vocational education system as an economic development tool to attract and maintain employers.

Francis Tuttle, founded in 1982, serves the northwest section and a small southwest section of Oklahoma City. Since its inception, Francis Tuttle has offered traditional preemployment vocational and technical training to secondary students as well as employer-based training to businesses and industries in the area. The school enrolls 1,078 students in its traditional programs; 3 to 5 percent of these students are employed in local industries. In the last two years, Francis Tuttle has served nearly two hundred employers.

When the school was founded, it consisted of one building designed to house the traditional day program for preemployment students. In 1985 Francis Tuttle built the High Technology Center to provide high-technology training to traditional students. Area employers quickly recognized the quality and success of training provided at the center and began to request its training for their employees. Responding to heightened employer demand, Francis Tuttle built a Business and Industry Center to specifically meet the needs of area businesses. This center conducts:

• Small business management courses
• Customized courses conducted at employer locations
• Business and management training assessments (employers

identifying a general need for training receive assistance on specific training options and start-up capabilities)

- A bid assistance program including a computer data base (Employers receive assistance on securing government contracts. Francis Tuttle helps employers fill out government forms and wade through red tape and also monitors contract performance. As a result of this service, Oklahoma business revenues from government contracts have increased approximately 80 percent.)

Francis Tuttle had worked with Fred Jones Manufacturing Company in past years to provide supervisory and managerial training programs, and representatives from Fred Jones serve on Francis Tuttle's advisory board. It seemed a natural step in 1987 for Fred Jones to turn to Francis Tuttle for help with designing and delivering SPC and gauge control systems training.

Francis Tuttle's first step was to conduct a training assessment to determine what training programs were needed, how they would best be accomplished, and how they could be implemented through cooperation and coordination of resources. This resulted in a delineation of responsibilities for Francis Tuttle and Fred Jones. Francis Tuttle's job was twofold: to develop training and to act as a consultant in implementing training and SPC and gauge control procedures. Fred Jones was responsible for hiring a training coordinator who would continue the program after Francis Tuttle finished the beginning phases.

Training began in March 1987 and continued through January 1988. Over four hundred employees attended SPC classroom training at the employer site. The High Technology Center conducted four one- to three-hour classes per week. When the trainer was not teaching in the classroom, he assisted trainees "on the floor" with applying classroom learning on the job.

The results of the training program were overwhelmingly positive. General Motors recognized the improvements in the production process and sent Fred Jones unsolicited new contracts. Trainees revealed through evaluation reaction sheets that the training had a favorable impact on their job performance and satisfaction. This claim was confirmed by production-level evaluations done before and after training. As a direct result of employee training, Fred Jones reduced its test stand rejection rate by up to 50 percent (Kelly Sloan, telephone interview, September 1988; Ernie Morris, telephone interview, October 1988).

Proprietary Schools

Proprietary schools are private, for-profit schools that specialize in a particular trade or field. As a whole, these schools are not extensively involved in employer training, although some innovative secretarial schools may offer a variety of workshops, seminars, and custom courses on upgrading clerical skills, team building, time management, and goal setting for all levels of employees.

A Snapshot: Texas Instruments and Executive Secretarial School. Texas Instruments (TI) is a $5.5-billion company manufacturing semiconductors, defense systems and electronics, computer hardware and software, consumer products, and intelligent automation products. It employs 75,000 workers nationwide. In 1986 TI made the decision to shut down one of its divisions — a decision that would have dislocated 200 technical assembly workers.

To avoid such dislocation, Texas Instruments decided to offer those 200 workers retraining to move them into nontechnical positions within the company. Because of prior training experiences with the Executive Secretarial School, TI contacted them to train TI's 200 technical workers for nontechnical work.

The Executive Secretarial School (ESS), a one-year secretarial school located in Dallas, Texas, provides education to approximately 400 students and does a quarter of a million dollars worth of business annually providing training to local employers.

For twenty-nine years ESS has offered a broad range of services to employers. ESS assists employers with all phases of training from needs analysis to evaluation. All training services are coordinated by a three-person team and are conducted at the employer's site.

Every course done by ESS is customized or tailored. For example, a business writing course is crafted to meet the specific needs of the client. ESS trains many different types and levels of employees, including support staff, doctors, dock workers, security guards, and managers. Training programs range from business writing, telephone etiquette, and word processing to teamwork, leadership, stress management, and assertiveness training.

ESS maintains a high-visibility profile with area employers by using a combination of resources. First, employers are represented on the ESS Board of Directors and Advisory Board. Second, ESS operates a placement center that puts it in direct contact with employers. ESS also distributes brochures and other promotional information to alumni, who in turn pass this information on to their employers. Finally, ESS sponsors an annual public seminar to discuss a particularly current theme or topic affecting potential clients.

ESS designed and delivered a two-week training program for the 200 Texas Instruments technicians who would have been laid off. Training was conducted on the company site. Employees were divided into four groups and were trained in clerical skills, building self-esteem, how to use an adding machine, English, office and telephone etiquette, and filing skills. After training, TI placed 65 percent of the employees in office positions and 10 percent in nonoffice positions such as security guards and other upgraded positions; 5 percent to 10 percent were sent by TI to additional training courses (Jan Friedheim, telephone interviews, January 1988 and July 1988).

Trade and Professional Associations

Trade and professional associations are nonprofit and for-profit membership organizations that represent individuals in a particular area of expertise. They are governed by a board of directors and often have local chapters throughout the United States that operate under the bylaws and guidelines of the national organization. Professional and trade associations offer a wide range of services to their memberships. Many develop communication materials that discuss current trends and innovations, operate a government relations component that communicates with the U.S. Congress or state governments on relevant issues, and sponsor nationwide conferences to provide a forum for exchanging and updating new advances in their fields.

Of the 20,076 associations in operation in the United States, approximately 3 percent provide training as part of some kind of certification program; employers find that certification associated with training promotes status and recognition not only to the industry but also to the company employees participating in such a program. Over 6 percent offer some type of training programs (extrapolated from Gruber, 1988). However, employers are often unaware of training available from professional and trade associations. Associations can provide a high degree of expertise and are up to date on the professions and occupations that they represent. However, employers find that associations can be fairly inflexible, offering only a specified number of classes on certain topics and not, as a rule, customized training.

A Snapshot: Erol's Incorporated and the American Automobile Association. Erol's Incorporated, best known for its video rental stores, also sells and repairs televisions, video equipment, and cameras. The company, headquartered in Springfield, Virginia, employs 4,000 people in 185 locations east of the Mississippi. Erol's reports $100 million in sales annually.

Erol's's business demands the continual transporting of products from one site to another. Therefore, the company maintains a fleet of vehicles and employs 160 drivers.

In the early 1980s, Erol's's automobile insurance reflected an extremely poor driving record on the part of its drivers; it had a loss ratio on its insurance of 498 percent. In addition, Erol's was rapidly expanding and had begun to purchase large trucks whose size dictated that drivers have specific skills to comply with U.S. Department of Transportation regulations.

This situation prompted the company's vice-president for loss prevention to identify two training needs. Drivers needed training in order first to bring down insurance costs and second to meet certification standards set by the federal transportation agency. Fortunately, the vice-president had extensive knowledge of outside resources and contacted the American Automobile Association — an outside provider with expertise and an excellent reputation for effective driver improvement training.

The American Automobile Association (AAA) is a nonprofit membership association founded in 1902 to protect the interests and rights of American car owners. AAA's membership consists of 156 local clubs, which operate independently; each is governed by a board of directors. AAA represents thirty million individual members.

The American Automobile Association is widely known for its expertise and effectiveness in training. The national office, located in Falls Church, Virginia, provides a wide variety of customized training programs to its members, its service contractors, and many other groups and individuals. Local clubs also provide varying degrees of training services, depending on the size of the club. According to the national office, AAA training services have increased dramatically over the last five years.

The cornerstone of AAA's training services is the train-the-trainer approach. AAA's Traffic Safety Department trains and certifies a "master instructor" and provides him or her with the materials to return to an organization to train other employees. For example, the AAA Automotive Engineering and Road Services Department provides an Automotive Hi-Tech Mechanics' Training program. AAA conducts on-site or near-site training for working mechanics who want to upgrade their knowledge about emission and engine management systems. Once the training is completed, AAA leaves behind training curricula and visuals so that the company can institutionalize the training. This program is of particular significance to those vocational-technical instructors who are professionally mandated to complete skill-upgrading courses to stay abreast in their professions; AAA's program provides a direct, accessible, and mobile answer to this need. Other AAA training topics include alcohol awareness, child safety, driver improvement, accident prevention, and risk management. AAA believes that training is a membership service; nominal fees are charged to cover training costs.

Because most of AAA's services are modified to meet the specific needs of the client, training locations are often selected by the client. Some of the training courses are accredited by universities.

The vice-president for loss prevention contracted with AAA for a one-week train-the-trainer course in accident prevention. The vice-president, in turn, trained 600 Erol's employees over a two-year period. Drivers attended two-day classroom training in small groups. The results of the training were overwhelmingly positive. In the five-year period following training, Erol's saved up to $161,000 per year in insurance premiums and had no lost-time accidents. In addition, Erol's received commendations from both their insurance company and AAA. Erol's has hired an in-house trainer who continues to provide training for its drivers in order to comply with federal regulations and maintain lower insurance rates. The company's first master trainer—the vice-president—continues to receive information from AAA on new training techniques and procedures (George Giek, telephone interview, November 1988; Frank Kenel, telephone interview, November 1988; Paul Kindschy, telephone interview, November 1988; William Pleasants, telephone interviews, January 1988 and November 1988).

A Snapshot: Aspen Systems Corporation and the American Management Association. Aspen Systems Corporation is a $30-million information management company located in Rockville, Maryland. This service company employs 350 workers and provides a broad range of library, reference, and clearinghouse services as well as specialized legal and medical information management services to its clients. One of the largest purchasers of Aspen's services is the federal government.

Because management is the focus of the company's business, Aspen Systems has a strong commitment to management training, particularly for employees with supervisory and management responsibilities. To this end, Aspen continually provides training by using outside providers such as professional associations, consultants, and local colleges. The company's in-house training role is twofold. First and most frequently, the company distributes training program catalogues and brochures that describe available training programs from outside providers. Employees, in turn, select programs of interest and, with the approval of their supervisors, receive training. Second, the company determines specific training needs and seeks an outside provider to design and deliver a comprehensive training program.

In 1988 Aspen Systems secured a large contract from the federal government for new services. This contract resulted in Aspen's hiring additional employees and integrating a new project team into its organizational structure. In addition, the company had been growing steadily over the past three years. New employees had been brought in, and existing employees had been brought up through the ranks. Because of this expansion and shifting of human resources, Aspen's top-level executives and upper-level managers began to face increasing difficulty when communicating between divisions and levels within the company.

In response to the communications problem, Aspen Systems decided to provide communications training to fifty mid-level managers. After reviewing training catalogues and literature, the director of human resources and training contacted the American Management Association — an association that had provided training to Aspen employees for seven years — for communications training.

The American Management Association (AMA) is an international nonprofit educational organization representing approximately seventy-five thousand individual and corporate members. AMA international offices are located in Belgium, Brazil, Canada, and Mexico; domestic offices are located in Atlanta; Boston; Chicago; New York; San Francisco; and Washington, D.C. The association also maintains a conference center in Hamilton, New York, and a support center in Saranac Lake, New York.

Management education is the cornerstone of AMA membership services; the association has been conducting training since its inception in 1923, when it was founded to improve the field of management. Today AMA provides members with a wide range of customized and generic training programs as well as prepackaged training materials such as videotapes, multimedia kits, audiocassettes, and home study courses. All programs focus on major issues facing today's managers.

The AMA employs 750 workers around the world and calls on an additional 1,500 stand-up training speakers and leaders to supplement that staff. Each year the association trains approximately 170,000 managers. About 12,000 to 15,000, or approximately 10 percent of those managers, participate in onsite, customized courses.

The AMA informs its members of available training services by distributing catalogues several times a year. In addition, the organization advertises its training services by direct mail and in professional and business publications.

In 1988 Aspen Systems contracted with AMA to provide a one-day communications training program for fifty mid-level managers. Aspen Systems' director of human resources and training worked with AMA to tailor the program, called "Communicate to Get the Response You Want." AMA then twice delivered the one-day training program at Aspen headquarters, each time to a group of twenty-five mid-level managers.

Both executives and mid-level manager trainees felt the impact of the training program. For Aspen executives interagency communication became less strained, enabling decisions to be carried through more efficiently and effectively between as well as within agency divisions. Mid-level managers reported less difficulty in completing tasks and a clearer understanding of how communication skills affect day-to-day management-employee relations.

Aspen Systems Corporation plans to continue circulating AMA training catalogues and brochures to its employees and, when the need arises, to contract with AMA for customized training (Donald R. Taylor, telephone interview, September 1988; Jacklyn Matrigali, telephone interview, October 1988).

Unions

Unions and employers are two naturally dependent entities that have regularly created linkages. Unions have traditionally taken several different avenues to ensure that their membership is provided with the most current techniques available to perform on the job. The path a union chooses, however, is governed in part by the power it holds in controlling the employers' ability to hire employees outside the union membership. For example, unions that control the labor supply usually provide job-specific training to members. Employers, in turn, hire only employees who have completed union training programs. Unions that do not have the power of sole supplier of the employer's labor pool are often less vigorous about training. They provide training to some individuals who are then given preference by employers during the hiring process.

Still other union organizations use training to strengthen unity and cohesiveness in order to maintain a strong presence in the workplace. These unions, through their education departments, provide basic education, training to facilitate participation in the governance of the union, and basic political education to union members, most of which is not job specific. Often the purpose of such training is to make union members more aware of union concerns, enhance negotiation skills, or provide leadership skills.

The newest training arrangements, and those that embody both missions—to keep skills current and thus remain employable and to support a group presence in the employer community—are those negotiated by unions in union contracts and funded jointly or administered jointly with the employer. The UAW-Ford joint training program was the first such program developed in 1982, and several other unions have followed suit.

A Snapshot: Chrysler and the United Auto Workers. Chrysler is a $22.5-billion automobile-manufacturing company headquartered in Highland Park, Michigan. The company employs 100,732 employees in the United States in thirty-five plant locations. Chrysler's training system is decentralized, with each of the corporate divisions responsible for its own training programs. The in-house training staff is large and is supplemented by outside training providers. The company offers training programs to virtually every kind of employee; training programs range from marketing, sales, quality, technical, dealership, and vendor training to supervisory, management development, and executive development programs.

In 1985, during contract negotiations between Chrysler and the United Auto Workers (UAW), the company identified a new training need. The union wanted to offer additional training programs to its membership, including programs that would improve job security and product quality, and to retrain displaced workers for new employment opportunities. Chrysler recognized that by investing in the programs the union was seeking, it would actually be investing in a skilled work force that would ultimately improve the company's competitive edge. Therefore, Chrysler and the United Auto Workers established a Joint Activities Board to fund, implement, and administer such training initiatives.

The Joint Activities Board is composed of three union representatives and three management representatives. The vice-president of human resources and the director of the Chrysler Department of the UAW serve as cochairmen of the board. A National Skills Development and Training Committee carries out the functions of the board.

The Joint Activities Board sponsors a number of activities in addition to training, including a child care program, alcohol and drug abuse programs, an attendance program, and a relocation assistance program, to name a few. Training programs sponsored by the board include a tuition assistance program (TAP) and a technical preparation program, which offers reinforcement training in preparation for more advanced and complex technological training, technical training, human relations training, team building, decision making, group organization, and hazard communication and safety training. All activities of the Joint Activities Board are housed in the National Training Center.

The joint training program, implemented in 1986, is designed so that each plant location develops tailored programs geared to the needs of the employees at that specific plant. Local committees implement the goals of the Joint Activities Board and determine what activities and training programs will take place in the plant. These committees also have the autonomy to distribute their local funds as they see fit. Educational training counselors (ETCs) are also an important part of each local program. They are employed at each plant site to help each worker develop an individual training plan. This ensures that each employee gets the training needed for her or his job.

Funding for the joint training program comes from contributions from both UAW and Chrysler (usually equal to five cents per hour worked per employee). The contributions are placed in three funds: the National Fund, which is used for national programs; the Local Fund, which supports activities in each plant; and the Reservoir Fund, which is used for special projects and to supplement other funding sources (UAW/ Chrysler National Skill Development and Training Center).

Community-Based Organizations

Community-based organizations (CBOs) are formed around a central theme or issue and represent a particular group or population. Most CBOs operate on shoestring budgets ranging from $15,000 to $200,000. Because these organizations mainly deliver public job-training programs, employers might not directly link to CBOs; employers instead usually link directly with a public job-training entity and its administrators, who then subcontract with the CBO.

Employers that do link directly with community-based organizations find that they are flexible and, in many cases, willing to customize training. In addition, the nonprofit tax status of CBOs greatly reduces employee training costs for employers.

A Snapshot: Comcast Cablevision of Philadelphia, L.P., and the Philadelphia Opportunities Industrialization Center. Comcast Cablevision of Philadelphia, L.P., is an affiliate of Comcast Corporation. The corporation, which effective the third quarter of 1988 had revenues of $327 million and assets of $1.6 billion, employs 3,800 workers. Comcast Corporation is principally engaged in management, development, and operation of cable communications systems serving approximately 2.5 million subscribers nationwide. Included in this number are approximately 1.1 million subscribers served by affiliates whose financial condition and results of operation are not consolidated with those of Comcast Corporation. Additionally, the company provides cellular telephone communications as well as sound and music services. The class A common stock and the class A special common stock of Comcast Corporation are traded in the over-the-counter market and are reported in the National Market List under the NASDAQ symbols CMCSA and CMCSK, respectively.

Comcast Cablevision of Philadelphia, L.P. (herein referred to as Comcast), serves subscribers in northeast and northwest Philadelphia, Pennsylvania, and employs three hundred workers at two local franchises. A large number of Comcast's employees are field technical workers who require specialized training to perform a specific skill such as cable installation and troubleshooting in addition to operating high-technology cable equipment.

The city of Philadelphia recognized the employment and financial benefits Comcast would bring to the city. Comcast would be hiring employees from the local area as well as initiating service and training contracts with other companies and service organizations within the city. As a provision of its negotiated franchise agreement, Comcast proposed that a local community-based organization be designated as one of its training providers. The city accepted and supported this provision of the proposal.

Comcast uses a full range of resources to provide training for its employees. First, the company maintains an in-house training department consisting of one full-time training manager assisted by other managers in areas directly related to their field. Second, Comcast contracts with consultants as well as equipment manufacturers and suppliers for customized and prepackaged training programs. Finally, the company, as part of its negotiated franchise agreement with the city of Philadelphia, contracts with a local community service organization—the Philadelphia Opportunities Industrialization Center (OIC)— for preemployment and other training, as necessary.

By 1988 OIC had successfully provided a six-week preemployment training program to thirty people during Comcast's start-up phase. Comcast had hired eleven of the thirty trainees and had since been satisfied with their performances on the job. Based on their successful training partnership and their rapidly expanding work force, Comcast contacted the Philadelphia OIC to design and deliver additional customized training.

The Philadelphia Opportunities Industrialization Center is a nonprofit, community-based organization serving disadvantaged and special populations. The Philadelphia OIC was founded in 1964 to combat discriminatory, racial hiring practices by local companies. Noting the struggle of its clients to gain employment, the OIC recognized that many of its constituency lacked the skills necessary to enter the job market. The OIC immediately moved to remedy this inequity and initiated preemployment training programs for disadvantaged and minority populations. Over the past twenty-five years, the OIC had fine-tuned its training role in the Philadelphia area. It positioned the organization as an administrative training entity, bringing together available community resources to provide comprehensive training services to meet constituent and employer needs. In addition, the OIC expanded its training constituency to include special populations and its training services to include customized training for area employers. To date, the OIC customized employer training has reached approximately 150 employees in six businesses within the Philadelphia area.

The OIC's firm positioning within the community is due, in part, to extensive networking efforts such as advisory panels, which establish ties to all community resources, including local government, educational institutions, other nonprofit community organizations, businesses, and individual residents. Additionally, the OIC advertises all of its services, including training, through selected mailings of pamphlets and brochures.

The Philadelphia OIC and its staff of fifty serve as a model for eighty-one domestic and sixteen international sister organizations. Each of these sister organizations is an OIC affiliate and has the autonomy to develop its own programs according to the needs of the community in which it is located. A meeting once a year brings all of the affiliates together to share ideas and develop new initiatives.

In 1988 Comcast Cablevision contacted the Philadelphia OIC to provide a customized training program to its technical employees. The OIC took on an administrative role and served as the primary contractor. OIC responsibilities included securing a provider with expertise in training cable service technicians, monitoring training quality on site, and coordinating communications between all parties involved. The subcontractor—Temple University—provided a faculty member to develop and deliver the Comcast training program and certified trainees upon completion of the program.

OIC-Temple University delivered classroom training to seventy technical employees at the Comcast Cablevision site. Employees were trained in six classes, four lasting four weeks and two lasting two weeks. The classes were originally designed for service technicians, although cable installers and line technicians also participated. All of the employees who successfully completed the course were given a certificate from Temple.

Comcast was satisfied with OIC's training and is discussing future needs. The OIC continues to submit bids and seek opportunities for meeting the training needs of area employers (Robert Nelson, telephone interview, September 1988; Edward Miller, telephone interview, September 1988; Delores Muldrew, telephone interview, November 1988).

Federal Government

The federal government and its agencies, including the military, frequently develop training technology that, with some modification, could transfer to the private sector. Because large amounts of federal funds are spent developing these training technologies, Congress is beginning to consider making them available to private and public training entities. Employers may find that training programs designed by the federal government are very useful because they have been well researched and extensively tested.

A Snapshot: General Motors and the U.S. Department of the Army. General Motors (GM) is a $96-billion automobile manufacturer and electronics, aviation, and defense company headquartered in Detroit, Michigan. The company has approximately 160 plant locations in the United States and employs over 380,000 workers nationwide.

Training is a large part of General Motors' operation. Although the training is decentralized, the corporate training staff recommends training programs to its plants and departments and makes resources available to help those groups conduct training.

Recently, General Motors decided to scale down its operations. At the same time, the company moved to bring new technology into the workplace. GM recognized that training was necessary for employees to use the new technologies, and it designed a training program. However, when GM began to train employees in the new technological processes, another training need emerged. Many trainees lacked the basic skills to participate in the training program.

By 1986 the company decided that it needed to provide basic skills training to approximately 100,000 employees in GM plants throughout the United States. Because the training population was so large, GM wanted to guard against participants' being pulled off the line en masse for training. More specifically, the company wanted a computerized self-paced training program. As the search for resources began, the GM government affairs office in Washington, D.C., sent corporate headquarters information on a successful basic skills program designed by the Department of the Army. This program—the Job Skills Education Program (JSEP)—was perfect for GM; it was geared specifically toward training a large population in basic skills. GM immediately contacted the U.S. Department of the Army for assistance.

The Army Job Skills Education Program (JSEP) was developed by the United States Army with the help of Florida State University to train soldiers in the basic academic skills needed to perform their jobs. The program is designed for enlisted soldiers with rankings from E1 to E5 and skill levels of one or two and who receive a score of less than 100 on the General Technical Portion of the Armed Service Vocational Aptitude Battery.

The JSEP program is applicable to ninety-four of the most common jobs in the military. All of the jobs were analyzed to determine the skills essential to each. Roughly three hundred lessons were prepared, teaching over two hundred skills. The program is competency based, so soldiers learn only those skills needed for their jobs and for which they cannot meet the competency requirements. Soldiers must also take the lessons on skills pertaining to soldiers' common tasks — skills that every soldier is expected to know regardless of his or her job, including biological and nuclear warfare, code of conduct, and first aid.

The JSEP program was made available to the civilian sector as a result of recommendations by the Technology Transfer Task Force, composed of representatives from the Departments of Education, Labor, and Defense and from other groups. This task force looks at products in the public sector to see if they are useful to the private sector; the JSEP program was seen as potentially useful to employers.

Although the program has not been fully implemented in the private sector to date, Florida State has received a grant from the Department of Labor to study the transferability of the program to the civilian sector. One of the major issues in the study is the extent to which the lessons in the program need to be redesigned in a nonmilitary "degreening" context to be relevant to the civilian audience, to the costs involved, and to practical use by trainers. The program, both with and without a military context, is being tested in White Plains, New York.

Thus far the army has given the program to the state of North Carolina for use in vocational education programs and to Ford Aerospace and General Motors for use in their plants.

General Motors implemented the JSEP program in the first quarter of 1989. Before implementation, the company reviewed the material to identify potential problems with the program's military context. General Motors concluded that the military context did not pose a major problem. Because the program has only recently been implemented, the results are unknown. However, the company continues to explore the feasibility of linking other basic skills programs with JSEP. For example, individual GM plants are currently developing supplementary basic skills programs that are geared toward their local needs. These plants are in the process of identifying and assessing skill levels to determine the amount and level of basic skills training needed.

Business to Business

Companies often sell their training externally to other companies. This can occur in any industry, although it may be most extensive in the utility industry, where training programs are frequently exchanged. Utilities are in a unique situation in that they do not compete among one another; rather, they are monopolies within their local geographical regions.

The employers that utilize training offered by other employers are generally small and have a small or nonexistent central training department. These small employers usually purchase training from other employers in the same industry. One reason that this type of training exchange is limited is that employers selling programs externally usually do not vigorously market their products.

Securing training from another employer provides the purchaser with a safety net. If the business selling the training is reputable and is providing the same training to its own employees, the employer seeking training can be fairly certain that it is getting a quality program. The purchaser must keep in mind, however, that what works for the goose may not work for the gander — different environments and situations may produce differing results.

A Snapshot: United Technologies Corporation and Trans World Airlines. United Technologies Corporation (UTC), based in Hartford, Connecticut, provides a broad range of high-technology products and support services to the aerospace, building systems, and automotive industries. The corporation's best known products include Pratt & Whitney aircraft engines, Carrier heating and air-conditioning systems, Otis elevators and escalators, Sikorsky helicopters, Hamilton Standard aerospace systems, Norden defense systems, and UTC automotive components and systems.

United Technologies employs approximately 190,000 workers and operates about 300 plants and sales offices in fifty-seven countries. During 1988 the corporation realized a net income of $659 million based on sales of $18 billion.

Because of its international business focus — offices and plants as well as consumers for UTC products are located around the world — United Technologies owns ten corporate airplanes and employs approximately forty pilots.

Training is an integral function of airline ownership for the corporation. UTC is not alone in this approach, because flight crews must be certified and maintain proficiency in accordance with specific regulations set by the U.S. Federal Aviation Administration (FAA). In addition, rapid technological advances in aircraft systems and designs constantly pose new training challenges for aircraft personnel.

The airline industry acknowledges that aircraft training is a necessary, highly specialized and technical component of its industry. It requires trainers with highly specialized skills and access to expensive equipment such as flight simulators. Therefore, most aircraft owners, such as UTC, regularly train aircraft flight crews using outside resources.

The corporation's three-person in-house training department manages aircraft training for its flight crews. The department determines when training is needed, coordinates training schedules, and is responsible for standardizing training programs.

In 1976 United Technologies purchased a Boeing 727 to be used as a corporate aircraft. Since all previous flight crew training had been customized for other, smaller aircraft, and UTC had never owned a Boeing 727, the training department identified a need for 727 flight crew training. At that time, the company requested bids from airlines in the area. Trans World Airlines (TWA), well known within the industry as a training provider, was chosen to provide a comprehensive flight crew training program.

TWA is a Delaware-based airline serving both domestic and international routes through its hubs in St. Louis and New York. TWA's passenger service is its main source of revenue, but the airline also has a cargo service, provides training and maintenance contract services to a number of companies, and provides support services to airlines at several locations. TWA's total operating revenues for 1987 were over $4 billion. TWA employs approximately 30,500 workers and operates three training centers in the United States.

TWA has been offering its training programs to other employers for over twenty-five years; its various departments, all decentralized, sell approximately 10 percent of their training services externally. The total number of non-TWA employees trained by TWA varies widely from year to year. This number fluctuates according to scheduling constraints set by TWA and outside employer demand. One year TWA may train as few as fifty individuals from other companies, the next year as many as three hundred.

TWA offers a wide variety of training services for employers. Programs range from teaching trainees how to use new aircraft equipment, systems, and procedures—these programs may be prepackaged or customized—to dry lease agreements, where a company designs and delivers its own program using TWA training facilities and equipment. All training is conducted on TWA's training sites, where expensive training equipment such as flight simulators is located.

TWA does not market its outside training services. In all cases, companies who have contacted TWA have learned about its training services through "word of mouth."

UTC contracted with TWA to provide a comprehensive FAA-approved initial and recurrent training for all of its Boeing 727 crew members. The five-week initial training course consists of classroom training conducted by a stand-up instructor, flight simulator training and check ride, and a check ride in a Boeing 727 aircraft. Recurrent training is a three-day course consisting of general aircraft systems review in the classroom and twelve hours of simulator training and check ride. UTC's in-house training department coordinated pilot training schedules.

UTC and TWA continued to work together until United Technologies sold its Boeing 727 in 1988. Throughout the twelve-year period, TWA provided recurrent training to existing Boeing 727 flight crews and transition training to new pilots on the Boeing 727. UTC continues to work with other companies that provide crew training for its other aircraft (Ted Reiter, telephone interview, July 1988; Kenneth Kuhrt, telephone interview, October 1988).

Public Funding Sources and Intermediaries

The organizations listed above represent one type of provider — those that develop and deliver training. Two other players in the provider arena merit attention — those that underwrite (fund) employer training and those that act as intermediaries between employers and various training providers.

Providers that fund employer training programs generally use public funding sources. Providers that fund and deliver training are usually the administrative bodies of public job-training programs. Various public funding sources originate at the federal, state, and local levels.

Public Funds Generated at the Federal Level

The Job Training Partnership Act (JTPA) is the largest federal training program. From it, approximately $4 billion is divided annually among the states, distributed on a formula basis. The states then allocate the funds to localities, which have a great deal of autonomy in how the funding is spent on training.

There are two other pieces of federal legislation that offer incentives for employers to train. The Targeted Jobs Tax Credit (TJTC) is made available to employers that hire workers who are in certain targeted categories — usually those who fall below the federally determined poverty level. Employers receive a federal tax credit up to a specified amount when they hire employees who meet certain criteria. While the TJTC does not in fact have any training provisions, in effect it often results in training. Because training of the economically disadvantaged can be financed by other public job-training funds, TJTC can effectively lengthen the period of on-the-job training when another funding source expires.

The Veteran's Job Training Act also provides funds for a designated period to employers that hire and train veterans. All of these federal laws have restrictions on the populations that they serve.

Public Funds Generated at the State Level

There are also funding sources that originate at the state level, although, as with JTPA funds, they are likely to be distributed to localities, which then administer the funds under the guidance of the states. The funds are distributed by localities either directly to the employer, which will then conduct the training in house, or to a provider that has been contracted to do the training. In some states the vocational education system or the community college system is used as the training provider. In other states the funds may be distributed to other private or public institutions, such as CBOs, which then conduct the training.

State economic development funds may be the most common source of state funds for training. States are very interested in attracting employers as well as in providing incentives for employers to remain in the state. Forty-four states currently offer a number of economic incentives to attract businesses, including training incentives (Stevens, 1986). Some will only make training funds available to employers meeting specified criteria, such as being a growth industry, or to forestall an employer's proposing to move out of the state. Many times the funds are only available to employers that will be training special populations, such as low-income or dislocated workers.

There are as many different administrative structures developed for state economic development activities as there are states. However, each has funding sources, contracting arrangements, and targeted audiences.

Some states have established autonomous, quasi-public institutions to administer statewide job-training programs. The two most well known programs are the Massachusetts Bay State

Skills Corporation (BSSC) and the California Employment Training Panel (ETP). The ETP is funded by the equivalent of one-tenth of 1 percent of the excess state unemployment insurance; BSSC is funded by the state as well as by other public and private sources, including JTPA funds and Carl Perkins vocational education funds. This allows the BSSC to serve not only workers who have been in the work force for a number of years but also the disadvantaged population lacking the necessary skills to enter the work force.

The two programs are administered differently, although both are considered independent agencies. The BSSC is governed by a board of directors, and the ETP is governed by a panel, with its support services provided by the state Office of Economic Development. Both make funds available to businesses to provide training. BSSC requires a matching grant from the employer and does not have performance contracting. The ETP does not require matching funds but does follow a performance contract model that provides for payment of the grant as the employer or provider meets predetermined criteria. For example, the final 25 percent of the award may only be given when the trainees have been employed for a specified amount of time at a given wage.

A Snapshot: General Motors Corporation and the Industrial Commission of Ohio. General Motors Corporation is a $96-billion company primarily involved in the manufacture, assembly, and sale of automobiles, trucks, and automotive parts and accessories. In addition, the company manufactures defense and space products including turbine aircraft engines and communications systems. GM subsidiaries include Hughes Aircraft Company, Saturn Corporation, Electronic Data Systems Corporation, and Delco Electronics Corporation.

The General Motors automotive fabrication plant in Lordstown, Ohio, employs 2,400 hourly employees and 250 salaried employees. Safety training is institutionalized throughout GM. The automotive industry is heavily regulated by the federal government, and the Lordstown plant is therefore extremely concerned about safety requirements.

In 1983 GM at Lordstown decided to implement a new safety training concept that involved formalizing its training under the leadership of a joint union-management committee. The company determined that while it had employees with the necessary knowledge to deliver safety training, these employees lacked stand-up training skills. Therefore, GM decided to seek help from an outside provider that could conduct train-the-trainer courses for those employees most knowledgeable in safety topics. These employees, in turn, would deliver formal safety training to all plant employees.

Once the company had determined the extent of its training needs, it was easy to decide which outside provider to use. The company immediately contacted the Industrial Commission of Ohio—a governmental entity that had worked extensively with GM on safety training in the past.

The Division of Safety and Hygiene of the Industrial Commission of Ohio is responsible for providing accident and illness prevention services to employers within Ohio. The division provides only training and consulting services; it has no compliance powers. All training and consulting services are funded through 1 percent of the worker's compensation funds collected by the state of Ohio from every employer with one or more employees. Thus, for employers these services are considered prepaid; they do not pay each time they request training.

The Division of Safety and Health offers over three hundred hours of short-term training, both customized and packaged, to Ohio employers each year. Training services are developed and delivered by a staff of over two hundred consultants located in seven district offices around the state. This staff is composed of industrial and construction consultants, engineers, employee assistance professionals, ergonomists, and industrial hygienists. Customized training services are based on specific employer needs; the safety and hygiene staff work in concert with the employer and then conduct the training at the company's site.

On July 1, 1989, the division created the Ohio Center for Occupational Safety, which conducts multiday in-depth seminars and workshops for all employers and employees, focusing on issues such as industrial noise, safe welding, and industrial hygiene. These programs are listed in a course catalogue distributed to all Ohio employers.

The division's employer consultative services include:

- Team approach consultative services — division representatives go to a company site (on the employer's request) and help the employer correct health and safety problems through engineering, ergonomics, industrial hygiene, employee assistance, and inspection and training methods
- A resource center that houses information on training programs as well as state and federal health and safety regulations
- A research and statistics service that conducts analyses of costs and the nature of accidents occurring within a particular plant or industry group or statewide

After receiving the call from GM, three division staff members went on site to the Lordstown plant to develop and deliver a three-day train-the-trainer program for forty-five union (UAW) and management personnel. These forty-five individuals would eventually conduct formal safety training programs for plant personnel. Three courses were offered with fifteen people in each. The courses showed GM "trainers" how to put together a program and deliver it. After the three-day seminar, each participant left with outlines for training programs that could be further developed and put into place.

Both GM and the division benefited from this partnership. GM "master trainers" now deliver ongoing required training to all Lordstown plant employees. In addition, GM now has two safety training committees. The maintenance committee represents the maintenance area of the plant; one person from each trade is a member of the committee. The committee meets every week to plan training. One week out of the month, trainers conduct mandatory training for all members of the maintenance area. The second committee represents all other areas of the plant. One representative from each area is a member of the committee. The committee also meets once a week to plan training and sets aside one week a month (also mandatory) to deliver training for everyone in the plant. In both of these cases, each employee attends a half-hour training seminar. An entire area of the plant is shut down for that period so that everyone can attend.

While the results of the training have not been formally measured, GM contends that attendance, awareness of safety issues, and input from employees at the training programs have increased dramatically. Employees receiving training believe that the training is more professional and comfortable: it is held in a quiet, air-conditioned training room rather than on the shop floor. Last, both management and union representatives have reported that this effort has helped to increase cooperation between labor and management (John Paulson, telephone interview, September 1988; Raymond Hickman, telephone interview, March 1989).

Public Funds Generated at the Local Level

Many times, state funds are combined with local funds to provide training at the local level. In fact, most actual training activities take place at the local level. It is also at this level that federal JTPA funds are administered and frequently mixed with state resources such as funds designated for economic development. In addition, many localities may conduct and fund their own economic development activities, including a training component, in much the same way as do the states.

Conclusion

There has been some controversy concerning the way governments provide training to employers. The most common criticism is that public funds are being used to subsidize training for which the private sector should pay — and which it would finance in the absence of these programs. Public funds traditionally have been used to provide services that the private sector was unwilling or unable to provide. The notion of public funds being used to subsidize private ventures appears to run contrary to the intent of the legislation that created these funding programs. However, an important question to ask is whether or not the private sector would train special populations (low-income and dislocated workers, for example) in the absence of public funds. Perhaps they would, but these public funds may act as a motivator for employers to be more extensively and effectively involved in the training of these populations.

CHAPTER 6

Selecting and Using Providers for Different Types of Training

When employers enter into partnerships with outside providers, they may seek shortcuts that help overcome inherent obstacles created by cooperative arrangements. One distinguishing characteristic of employer-provided linkages is that they are constructed to meet the needs of specific trainee populations within the employer institution. Research shows that employers select certain providers over others based on the type of training they are seeking. These providers are most often selected because they offer the best training alternatives for a particular occupational population. This chapter will map out employer-provider linkages according to types of training, discuss which providers are used most frequently for that training population, and look at barriers and evaluation needs in linkages.

Linkages Are Distinguishable by Type of Training

Table 22 provides an overview of linkages and lays the groundwork for discussion.

Executive Development. Executive development programs are geared toward executives and high-level managers who supervise other, lower-level managers, have profit-loss responsibilities, and set organizational objectives.

Most large employers have executive development programs. At least two-thirds of those companies describe executive development programs as "individual development" or "the building of leaders." This program focus distinguishes executive development training from other employer-provided training programs. Executive employees are not provided training to help them perform a specific task more efficiently. Perhaps most employers take this stance because by the time employees reach the executive ranks, they have already benefited from extensive human capital development. As they moved through the ranks, these employees received both job-specific training and substantial professional development experiences, including traditional schooling, job rotation, and mentoring, that prepared them for higher management. Executive development programs are geared toward helping executives visualize the bigger picture—company direction, a company's domestic and international competitive positions, and the leadership role and responsibilities of the executive.

In most cases, executive development training programs are bought from outside providers. This conclusion is supported by research that shows that in-house training departments that administer executive development programs tend to be small, with only a one- or two-person staff. This staff is responsible for making contacts with providers and for coordinating and administering the employer side of the linkage. For example, staff identifies training needs, locates providers, and then selects or recommends appropriate programs, collects information regarding their applicability, and determines the future benefits of that linkage. In addition, most executive development programs are generic and do not need to be customized or tailored to particular company needs or skills. The company can therefore save time and resources by purchasing an existing program from an outside provider.

Universities, graduate schools, and quasi-educational institutes are the most commonly used providers for executive development training.

Management Development. Unlike executives, a manager executes policy rather than sets it. The manager is a "translator" who conveys policy and motivates the work force toward achieving company goals. Managers are responsible for supervising

Table 22. Overview of Employer-Provider Relationships.

Type of Training	Description of Trainee Population	Focus of Training	How Provider Is Used
Executive development	High-level managers and executives responsible for other, low-level managers; those who have profit-loss responsibilities and set organizational objectives	Consciousness raising on current global issues such as competitiveness, leadership skills	Develop comprehensive training programs — often generic
Management development	Managers responsible for lower-level managers and other employees	Basic management skills such as leadership, financial management, performance feedback, communication	Develop and deliver customized and tailored programs
Supervisory training	Supervisors responsible for managing other employees but not other managers	Basic management skills such as time management, communication, interpersonal, team building	Develop and deliver customized and tailored programs; supply training materials for in-house programs
Nontechnical professionals	Degreed workers who attain specialized expertise and have careers focused in that area	Upgrading professional skills such as business writing, team building; upgrading personal skills such as communications, goal setting	Develop comprehensive training programs when certification is included; develop and deliver customized and tailored programs
Technical professionals	Degreed workers who need grounding in state-of-the-art theory as well as applied knowledge	Upgrading academic knowledge, industry-specific applications of new theoretical knowledge	Develop comprehensive training programs — often generic

Table 22. Overview of Employer-Provider Relationships, Cont'd.

Training Program Format	Degree of In-House Training	Most Common Provider	Secondary Providers
Seminars/ workshops	Mostly outside	Universities, graduate schools, institutes	Small and large consultants, professional and trade associations
Seminars/ workshops	Mostly inside	Small and large consultants	Universities, community and junior colleges, professional and trade associations
Seminars/ workshops	Mostly inside supplemented by outside	Small and large consultants	Universities, community and junior colleges, professional and trade associations
Seminars/ workshops	The more specialized the training, the more outside; most often a balance between inside and outside	Small consultants	Large consultants, colleges and universities, community and junior colleges, proprietary schools, trade and professional associations
Seminars/ workshops	Mostly inside	Universities	Professional associations, R&D institutes

Table 22. Overview of Employer-Provider Relationships, Cont'd.

Type of Training	Description of Trainee Population	Focus of Training	How Provider Is Used
International (language and culture)	Upper-level managers, employees, and their families; applies to U.S. employees stationed abroad, foreign employees stationed in the U.S., reentry of U.S. and foreign citizens into domestic environment	Foreign language skills; social and professional skills in company culture and foreign culture	Develop comprehensive customized programs
Sales	Employees responsible for selling products and services to individuals and institutions	Product knowledge, motivation, sales techniques	Provide generic, prepackaged training materials to supplement inside programs
Safety	Employees dealing with hazardous materials or in hazardous situations	Conduct in potentially hazardous conditions	Provide generic training materials
Regulatory	Employees in industries governed by specific laws and regulations	Federal, state, and local law compliance	Develop comprehensive programs
Customer Service	Employees who have regular contact with employer's customers	"Smile" training, personal management, procedural training	Provide generic, prepackaged programs; develop and design new programs
Clerical	Support staff and employees with administrative and production responsibilities	Clerical and administrative skills; personal skills such as teamwork, interpersonal, communication	Provide and deliver generic, prepackaged programs—often tailored
Technical and Skills	Technicians, craft, and skill workers; employees who need specific expertise to perform one or more components of their jobs	Skills training to perform a specific function or set of functions	Develop and deliver comprehensive programs

Table 22. Overview of Employer-Provider Relationships, Cont'd.

Training Program Format	Degree of In-House Training	Most Common Provider	Secondary Providers
Short intensive courses, seminars/workshops, debriefings	Mostly outside	Small and large consultants	Universities and colleges, community colleges, trade and professional associations
Seminars/ workshops	Product-specific training mostly inside; sales techniques frequently outside	Large consultants	Community colleges, vocational schools, community-based organizations, unions
Embedded in job-specific training	Mostly inside	Small and large consultants	Community colleges, vocational schools, community-based organizations, unions
Seminars/ workshops	Mostly inside	Small and large consultants	Professional associations, institutes, colleges and universities
Seminars/ workshops	Mostly inside	Small and large consultants	Colleges, proprietary schools
Seminars/ workshops	Mostly outside	Small and large consultants, community colleges	Vocational schools, proprietary schools, professional and trade associations
Embedded in job-specific training	Balanced between inside and outside	Vocational-technical schools, community colleges	Small and large consultants, unions, trade associations

other employees, some of whom may be lower-level managers or supervisors. Managers frequently have concrete data to work with when undertaking a task and often have the most interaction with other employees in the organization.

Most employers believe that a company "makes" managers through extensive formalized training, on-the-job training, and mentoring. Therefore, management development training is not only common among American employers but is usually conducted within the parameters of company philosophy and culture (in house).

Most employees who become managers move from a technical expertise area to a managerial area, where they must take on new responsibilities such as coordinating resources and people. Therefore, employer-provided programs focus on basic management skills such as team building, budgeting, decision making, leadership, and communication.

When an employer does seek an outside provider, it generally does so to supplement its in-house efforts. Outside providers are most commonly used to develop and deliver seminars and workshops within the confines of employer design. Vendors and consultants have shown the most flexibility in this regard and are therefore the primary providers. In the case where an employer does not have inside resources to develop a management training program, or where it is not cost-effective to do so, managers are usually enrolled in generic seminars provided by colleges or universities, professional associations, or community colleges.

Supervisory Training. Supervisors are responsible for managing other employees but not other managers. Supervisors implement company policies at the point of production or service delivery and train other workers, whether as an overt part of their jobs or through subtle behavioral cues that signal their preferred methods of operation.

Most companies provide supervisory training in the same context as they do management development training. Supervisors usually come into their positions with technical expertise but lack the wide range of interpersonal and managerial skills required for supervisory positions. In addition, the direction and importance placed on those new skills are dictated by company culture and direction.

Supervisory training is therefore generally conducted in house and supplemented by outside resources. Programs focus on basic management skills such as team building, interpersonal skills, and communications. Employers who do not have the in-house resources to design and implement the training most frequently turn to vendors and consultants who have demonstrated the most flexibility in providing training within the confines of company culture. These providers may develop and deliver short seminars or may supply prepackaged training materials. Another commonly used option for these companies is to tap educational institutions such as universities and community and junior colleges as well as professional and trade associations. Such providers often provide generic seminars and workshops that meet employer needs.

Nontechnical Professionals' Training. Nontechnical professionals are degreed workers who have attained specialized expertise in areas other than mathematics and the sciences, for example, attorneys, writers, and personnel and training specialists. Nontechnical professionals generally have a great deal of autonomy in their jobs and are expected to work with a minimum of direct supervision. They make decisions related to their own areas of expertise, create their own methods for achieving major goals, and set and meet objectives that contribute to achieving larger company goals.

Most companies encourage professional growth for nontechnical professionals through participation in professional societies, university teaching, or consulting. However, employers do provide formalized training for this occupational group to help them update professional skills and expertise, meet company needs arising from new projects, provide orientation to corporate goals and culture, provide hiring and retention incentives, and help manage stress and improve health. Therefore, most training programs encompass both professional and personal effectiveness skills such as business writing, team building, time and stress management, conflict intervention, and speaking and presentation.

The more unique the employer's training needs are, the more likely the employer will do training for nontechnical professionals in house. For example, highly specialized topics, such as updating certified public accountants on the latest tax laws, are more likely to be done in house with assistance from outside providers. The most commonly used outside provider under these circumstances is the small consultant; small consulting firms usually are known for their expertise in a specific area.

Technical Professionals' Training. Technical professionals are most frequently employees who hold a college degree or higher. They are educated and trained to make broad judgments, to invent, and to apply a particular intellectual discipline to problem solving. More specifically, technical professionals usually work autonomously and are responsible for developing new products and designs, conducting research, and making diagnoses and prescribing treatment (in the health care industry) but are not necessarily responsible for formal management or exercising direct authority over subordinates.

Most employer-provided training for technical professionals focuses on updating skills or knowledge to apply to new technologies. Seminars are usually geared toward a specialty area that can be broadly applied to a specific area of expertise. For example, a seminar for technical professionals might introduce a new synthetic material and explain its development, properties, and uses. One trainee — for example, the design engineer — who attends the training to develop a new product will use the information differently than another trainee — for example, the engineer — who will test the product once it is developed.

While most of this type of training is provided in house, employers frequently use colleges and universities because of their teaching approach and their R&D expertise. However, there are a growing number of R&D institutes as well as manufacturing companies that are coming into the training loop for technical professionals. They provide a new comprehensive focus because they bring together all workers involved in developing a new product — from technical professionals to production workers to sales and marketing personnel.

International Training. International training participants are generally upper-level managers, employees, and their families who are going to work or live in a foreign country. This description applies not only to U.S. citizens stationed abroad but also to foreign employees stationed in the United States.

Because international training encompasses such a broad spectrum, it has several components. International training includes short, intensive courses, seminars, and workshops in:

- Language training for U.S. employees stationed abroad and foreign employees stationed in the United States and for the families of these groups
- Culture training on the social and political environments for U.S. employees stationed abroad and foreign employees stationed in the United States and for the families of these groups
- Culture training on the business (company) environment to teach U.S. employees stationed abroad and foreign employees stationed in the United States how to function professionally
- Cultural reentry training for U.S. employees stationed abroad and foreign employees stationed in the United States and for the families of these groups to reorient and update them on social, economic, cultural, and professional climates in their native countries

Many companies provide international training out of necessity; their employees must be able to adapt and communicate in foreign surroundings to perform their jobs — very few employees and their families hold these skills before they are assigned to an overseas job. Because this type of training is so specialized, employers almost always seek outside providers to conduct it. For example, a company rarely employs an individual who not only is conversant in German, Japanese, or Spanish but also is well versed in the political, social, and economic postures of each of the countries where the language is spoken.

Employers generally contract with small and large consulting firms that specialize in this field for all types of international training. However, colleges and universities as well as professional and trade associations are beginning to break into this field. They have started to demonstrate to employers that they have qualified staff available on a continuing basis to provide comprehensive programs in this specialized training arena.

Sales Training. Sales training programs are geared toward employees responsible for selling products and services to individuals and institutions. While most of these employees work within the retail industry as salespeople, clerks, and cashiers, there are a large number of sales representatives in commodities, securities, and other service industries. Sales employees are usually integrated into the culture and structure of an organization and are responsible for relaying new product applications and innovations up the corporate ladder. In fiscal terms, business strategies often hinge on the strength of the sales force.

Because the connection between sales and the financial bottom line is clearly evident, most employers deem sales training essential and conduct the training in house. Sales training topics include product orientation and updates, interpersonal skills, negotiation, and general selling skills such as presentation, business writing, and telephone manner, usually presented in workshops or seminars.

Many employers use a blend of inside and outside resources, depending on the training topic. For example, product-specific sales training that deals with proprietary issues is often done in house. This is done not only to maintain a competitive edge but also because in-house staff are usually familiar with the product and readily available to deliver training. On the flip side, generic sales training on topics such as sales and motivation techniques is available from a variety of providers. Many are even available in the video market. It is much more cost-effective for the employer to purchase these training programs than to reinvent the wheel by having them custom made.

Large consulting firms are the most commonly used providers for sales training. Some companies link with colleges and universities to reward them for their merit to the company. In addition and less frequently, employers link with community colleges, professional and trade associations, and unions for sales training.

Safety Training. Safety training is geared toward employees who deal with hazardous materials or are in hazardous job situations. These employees must learn how to handle and operate products and equipment under potentially dangerous conditions.

Because safety training often deals with life-or-death situations for employees and citizens, most employers allocate in-house resources toward safety training. In addition, because its purpose is to prevent accidents, most safety training is embedded in job-specific training.

General topics in safety training include industrial hygiene, fire protection, and loss protection. Most safety training is not taught as separate courses; rather, it is incorporated into general courses. For example, safety instructions for climbing telephone poles or working on top of poles are not taught in separate classes; they are taught as part of a course on how to perform the job of a telephone line repairman.

Employers generally link with outside providers for safety training when they are providing a generic program such as first aid or they need supplemental program materials such as videotapes. These items are commonly available for purchase as off-the-shelf products.

Employers most frequently look to large and small consultants for assistance in these areas. Secondary providers include community colleges, vocational schools, community-based organizations, and unions.

Regulatory Training. Regulatory training is geared toward employees in industries governed by specific laws and regulations. In fact, training requirements are usually laid out in regulations issued by a government agency. These regulations usually include guidelines for how, when, and for how long training must be administered. It comes as no surprise, therefore, that this type of training is considered a must by the employer and that in-house resources are allocated for that purpose.

When an employer does seek assistance from outside resources, it is usually to provide and deliver generic or tailored program materials for workshops or seminars. Primary providers in this area are large and small consulting firms, followed closely by professional associations, institutes, and colleges and universities.

Customer Service Training. Customer service employees have regular contact with the employer's customers. They are the link between the company, the product, and the consumer; advertising may make the promises, but customer service workers must deliver on those promises.

Most employers believe that customer service employees must project a "company image" and be aware of the unique characteristics of their clientele. In addition, for many, a customer service job is a first job. Therefore, most employers regularly conduct customer service training with in-house resources. When training is provided by an outside provider, it is usually done within the confines of the organization's culture. Outside providers are frequently brought in when the employer is initiating a new program or when a specialized short seminar or workshop is needed. In many circumstances, outside providers are contacted to provide supplemental prepackaged materials for an in-house program.

Customer service training programs focus on interpersonal skills, product and service orientation, and customer-interaction skills—which range from learning how to be friendly to procedures for handling an irate customer.

When using an outside provider, most employers seek assistance from small and large consulting firms followed by community colleges and proprietary schools.

Clerical Training. Clerical workers include support staff and employees with administrative, production, and information management responsibilities. These employees have generally learned computer operation or a new word processing program within the past five years and now use a personal computer for preparing letters, keeping records, and scheduling office events. Many of today's clerical personnel are responsible for training new clerical workers and even professional staff on new office equipment.

Most organizations do not provide formal clerical training because they believe that clerical workers enter the work force with most of the basic skills that enable them to do their jobs. However, formal clerical training is increasing as technology drives clerical workers into a more professional stance in the business community. As this occurs, clerical training programs are beginning to focus on time management, conflict resolution, and interpersonal skills such as teamwork. This shift in focus has prompted formal skills training in production techniques, telephone etiquette, and office manners.

Organizations most frequently select large and small consulting firms and community colleges for formal clerical training. Other providers include vocational and proprietary schools and professional and trade associations.

Technical and Skills Training. Technical and skills training is geared toward technicians and craft and skill workers who require specific expertise to perform one or more components of their jobs. Often, these employees go through a certification process that recognizes their ability to perform a specific function on the job.

Because this type of training encompasses a broad range of workers, it is difficult to delineate clearly how employers sponsor their training. Overall, employers appear to strike a balance between in-house and outside resources. One fact is clear, however. Technical and skills training is generally embedded in job-specific training. When outside providers are used, they develop comprehensive programs that can be applied directly on the job. Outside providers employers use most frequently include vocational-technical schools and community colleges. Less frequently, employers look toward unions, trade associations, and small and large consulting firms.

Difficulties Encountered
When Establishing Linkages

Difficulties often surface when employers and providers attempt to establish linkages, but they are seldom insurmountable. In some cases, the employer may not get what it requested from the provider because of poor communication, lack of feedback mechanisms for monitoring the work of the provider, or lack of evaluation methods. Other difficulties may arise when a provider is not familiar with the specific needs and problems of a particular industry or organization. This problem may simply require extra time and effort on the part of the employer to orient the provider to the industry or organization.

Rarely do such problems erect barriers that prevent the establishment of linkages; rather, they may just drive a greater investment of time or other resources from the employer.

Evaluation of Outside Programs

Evaluation of programs conducted entirely or in part by outside providers would seem to be very important in helping the employer determine its return on the training investment. An effective evaluation system can ensure that the employer has received the product contracted from a provider. However, most employers do not utilize an effective evaluation system for in-house training; therefore, programs provided by outsiders are not evaluated any more thoroughly than are in-house programs. (See Chapter Three for more discussion on training evaluation according to trainee population.) Current evaluation methods consist mostly of informal worksheets measuring a trainee's reaction to the program. Follow-up sessions may occasionally be held to see if training was useful for trainees. This type of evaluation is usually very subjective.

Possibly more important than an evaluation that occurs after the fact may be continual monitoring by the employer of the provider's progress. Most employers do monitor providers to some extent, but the degree of monitoring is generally proportional to the amount of involvement between the employer and the provider. Like evaluation, monitoring tends to be informal and haphazard.

One process that may have built-in procedures for monitoring and evaluating training programs conducted by outside providers is the RFP. Because an RFP is a formal written agreement specifically outlining the roles of the employer and provider, more care may be taken by both parties to meet and evaluate the specifications contained in the RFP.

Building the Strategic Role of Training

CHAPTER 7

Organizational Strategies and Training Roles

Strategy: A Primer

The word *strategy* is from the Greek *strategos* and has its roots in military parlance. Literally translated as "the art of the general," it was originally used to describe the grand design behind a war or battle.

Today we think of strategy on many levels. Business has adopted the term and has applied it to concepts such as long-range planning and the management of resources needed to achieve the goals and objectives of such plans. Often short-term decisions that may have long-term effect are described as strategic. The term has even edged its way into everyday conversation, as individuals chart the tactics they will use to tackle a problem.

For the purposes of this chapter, we will rely on the traditional definition of strategy, adapted by business leaders and academicians from its military roots. Strategy, therefore, is here defined as the broad-scale plan for operating in a competitive environment to achieve organizational goals. It provides the overarching vision for implementing a successful campaign to realize goals, and it provides a backdrop for any number of tactical decisions that are made in pursuit of an ultimate goal. (Tactical decisions, in contrast, are the short-term actions designed to implement strategy, the gears that drive the broad-scale game plan toward success.)

159

For most organizations, there are at least two levels of strategy:

- *umbrella (organizationwide) strategies,* the long-term, overarching plans the business has for achieving success in the marketplace
- *functional (or divisional) strategies,* the operational plans that address the day-to-day practicalities needed to implement the overarching strategy

In large corporations that encompass multiple organizations or businesses, the parent organization may have a strategy that addresses the *entire* organization's health and welfare in the marketplace. In addition, each individual business that the corporation owns may have its own umbrella strategy that both addresses that entity's long-term goals and is compatible with the corporate strategy. The operational divisions of those individual businesses will have their functional strategies for effecting the umbrella strategy. The tools the functional units use to achieve organizational and functional strategies are tactics (see Figure 2).

While an unconscious approach to participation in the marketplace may yield temporary victories, only a well-thought-out strategy can result in sustained success. That is why over the last thirty years more and more organizations have begun to employ the strategic approach. Fueling this movement has been the realization that while management by intuition works in the short term, organizations generally cannot be managed successfully by relying solely on "seat-of-the-pants" decision making. Neither can they be run autocratically, following an inflexible set of rules.

Instead, successful organizations define their objectives, then set about developing an overarching game plan to pursue their goals. From this plan flow operational strategies and tactical decisions that move the organization toward its goals. The overarching plan provides the organization with a well-thought-out and clear picture of its basic approach to gaining the competitive edge. It also provides the organization with the flexibility

Figure 2. Functional Strategies and Tactics.

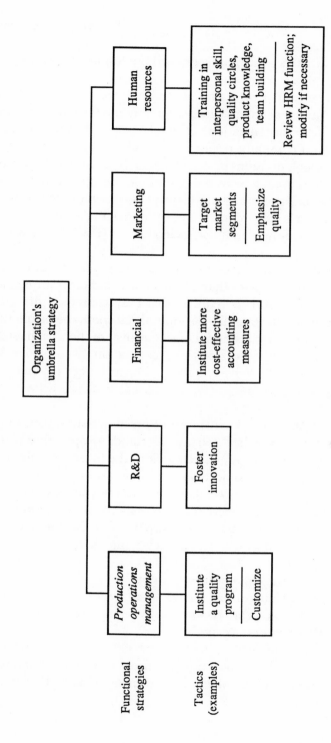

Functional strategies

Tactics (examples)

Organization's umbrella strategy

Production operations management

Institute a quality program
_____
Customize

R&D

Foster innovation

Financial

Institute more cost-effective accounting measures

Marketing

Target market segments
_____
Emphasize quality

Human resources

Training in interpersonal skill, quality circles, product knowledge, team building
_____
Review HRM function; modify if necessary

Source: Adapted from Pearce and Robinson, 1985.

to modify its tactical approaches without losing sight of the over-arching plan.

The marks of a strategic decision are that it is future oriented and that its implementation impacts the long-term prosperity of the organization. It involves the allocation of large amounts of company resources and affects many or all of the organization's divisions or departments. It hinges on the involvement of top managers in the planning processes and considers both the multiple (and frequently inconsistent) goals of the organization's stakeholders and the impact of external factors such as economic, labor, or societal shifts (Pearce and Robinson, 1985, pp. 7–8).

Adopting a strategic approach requires that managers think in broader terms than those for which their training often has prepared them. It requires that they view their organizations from a statesmanlike position, think about the big picture, and attempt to understand the perspectives of the various stakeholders inside and outside the organization.

Thomas L. Wheelen and J. David Unger captured the essence of this:

> They [top management] cannot make decisions based on long-standing rules, policies, or standard operating procedures. Instead, they must look to the future to plan organization-wide objectives, initiate strategy, and set policies. They must rise above their training and experience in such functional/operational areas as accounting, marketing, production or finance to grasp the overall picture. They must be willing to ask these key strategic questions:
>
> 1. Where is the corporation now?
> 2. If no changes are made, where will the corporation be in one year, two years, five years, ten years? Are the answers acceptable?
> 3. If the answers are not acceptable, what specific actions should the corporation undertake? What are the risks and payoffs involved? [Wheelen and Unger, 1986, pp. 4–5].

Together, the answers to these critical questions frame a picture of where the organization is today, where it will be in the future given its present strategy, and where it wants to be. The business school literature calls this a "gap analysis," and it is absolutely essential to strategic planning.

Successful strategic management can only occur if it is built on a broad base of knowledge about the organization and its capabilities. It cannot occur in the rarefied atmosphere of a board room; it must instead be built on the insights and creativity of people throughout the organization. Its centerpiece must be an overarching strategic plan underpinned by the collective input of the work force conveyed through their managers. All employees, but especially supervisors and managers, are environmental scanners, monitoring and interpreting data; managers serve to translate a diverse array of information that bubbles up around them into a coherent package of information for upper-level managers. "While the strategic process is certainly overseen by top managers — because they have a broad perspective on the company and its environment — there are multiple opportunities for managers at all levels to participate in various phases of the total process" (Pearce and Robinson, 1985, p. 15).

But there is the rub. While the opportunity for input may be afforded, the skill to provide that input may be absent.

The understanding of strategic concepts has become increasingly sophisticated at the top levels of organizations, but that sophistication has not filtered down throughout the layers of management and workers that are the implementing parts of the organization. In fact, how strategy is understood by top management and how the term is used in everyday conversation by the majority of middle managers, professionals, and line workers are often very different. The employees whose familiarity with the concept of strategy is limited to how it is used colloquially may find it difficult to understand the subtleties of the organizational strategic planning process.

Hopefully, this material, which provides a context for viewing strategy, will help break down the artificial barriers and confusion erected by the commonplace — and often cavalier —

usage of the term, placing in their stead new clarity and awareness. Toward that end, this chapter provides an overview of some common theoretical constructs for understanding the strategic management process. Its main focus, however, is a straightforward framework for analyzing a company's overarching (umbrella) and functional/operational strategies as well as understanding the tactics employed to achieve those strategies. Last, it sets the stage for Chapter Nine, which is a "how-to" guide for building the kind of coalitions and relationships needed to effectively influence strategic decision making.

Special thanks to John A. Pearce II, chairman of the Department of Management at George Mason University (Va.), School of Business Administration; his colleagues Debra Cohen, assistant professor of management, and Carolyn Erdener, assistant professor of management; and to Thomas J. Cosse, associate dean and director, E. Caliborne Robins School of Business, University of Richmond (Va.), for their assistance in the development of this analysis.

Why Should Training and Development Advocates/Professionals Think Strategically?

Training and development practitioners are, by and large, very good at what they do. They have defined their role as dealing with the humanistic part of the organization, the part charged with readying workers to assume new and increasing demands.

This is an admirable viewpoint, but in today's modern business environment it is insufficient for success. Training and development professionals must transform themselves into savvy, knowledgeable business people who not only are competent in their functional roles but also understand the overall framework in which their business operates.

Only with this understanding can training professionals gain the credibility to access the decision-making process inside a company. Only with a knowledge of strategic frameworks and company goals and strategies can the training professional help to develop the kind of organizationwide environment that recognizes the training professional as a major player on the organizational field.

All too often training and development are the caboose on the corporate train. Training discussions occur after an important capital or process decision is made. But, just like production or marketing, training is a profit and loss center (although management usually does not regard it as such because it does not *directly* generate revenues, and it does incur costs). The significant sums invested in a company's human capital can be better targeted by understanding its strategic direction and tactical thrust. Training professionals have a legitimate place at the table when strategic issues are discussed.

It is important to understand that training professionals will be less effective, as well as less valuable to an organization, if they are merely fire fighters. The role of fire fighter is familiar to most trainers. It is a role most often assigned to those outside the decision-making loop — to those who are challenged to figure out how the unexpected implications of a strategic decision can be met after the fact.

Every organization has its fire fighters, but they are largely expendable. In lean times their role is one that can be assumed by a substitute who can step in and hose down the flash fires. They are not viewed as part of the fabric of the organization, as essential as operations or sales. And so, in lean times, the fire fighters are the first to go.

Being part of the strategic loop means giving up the job of full-time fire fighter. The essence of the training function is to serve as a part-time fire fighter because the trainer is an organizational problem solver. But, as part of the strategic management process, that same professional will also be seen as an integral part of the organization's long-range picture.

However, to effectively link training and development with business strategies, human resource professionals must understand the thinking behind the strategic process. What is the organization's approach to strategic planning? Is there a particular strategic framework that the organization uses? Understanding can unlock the opportunity to affect the implementation of a strategy by bringing consideration of the human capital implications to the front.

Unfortunately, training professionals are generally not educated to think strategically. Most academic training for the relatively new discipline of human resource development has come from university adult education departments and has centered on learning theory, training methodology, and delivery methods. Strategic planning, a discipline of the business school, has not generally made the crossover to these human resource programs. In the few places where the human resource development program is under the auspices of a university business school, there is exposure to these concepts (and, as a matter of course, business school majors receive courses on strategic human resource management as part of their standard curriculum).

However, it is vitally important that each training professional understand the strategic design employed by his or her organization in order to be effective in serving that organization and developing its human capital. Otherwise, the training function is less effective as a tool for implementing growth and change.

Frameworks for Viewing Strategy

Efforts to construct a framework that can serve as a road map for the would-be strategic manager must begin with an understanding of the many points on the competitive compass. The strategic planning and management process is both static and dynamic. The grand schemes and overarching strategies of organizations lead to numerous operational and short-term decisions that cascade down toward the organization's implementers — its work force. To recognize the overarching notion is to be able to anticipate repercussions and to be able to move from a reactive posture in an organization to a proactive one.

The academic community has struggled for years to devise models that clearly and precisely communicate the concept of "strategizing." Books upon books have been written about strategic planning and management, and business schools have set about the task of training a legion of strategic players for the corporate playing field.

Out of this have come many models for *thinking about* organizational strategy, each enabling people to view the formulation and connection of overarching and functional strategies in different ways. Every strategic planner has her or his favorite variation on the strategic theme. Space does not permit a comprehensive analysis of all the many frameworks. What follows, however, is a look at six of the most commonly employed approaches.

The Boston Consulting Group: Strategic Matrix. One well-known strategy model is that developed by the Boston Consulting Group (BCG) under Bruce D. Henderson in the mid 1960s. BCG's approach is one example of a class of approaches referred to as "portfolio management planning." The portfolio approach allows an organization to examine each of its separate business units in terms of its contribution to the corporation's portfolio of businesses.

This framework uses a matrix that serves as a simplified vehicle for viewing the strategic process. It facilitates an organization's understanding of its market position by examining the market share and market growth rate of its products, and it suggests the most appropriate approaches for dealing within those parameters. Importantly, the matrix can be overlaid with the matrixes of competitors to provide a comprehensive picture of an organization's competitive posture.

This model has captured a place in the business vernacular by utilizing colorful descriptors to categorize strategic business units and their most likely strategies:

- The *question mark* business has a small market share, but, because the market is expanding rapidly, the organization's optimal strategy is to invest resources and increase its market share.
- The *rising star* business has a large market share in a rapidly growing market. Its best organizational strategy is to continue high investment and expand market share.
- The *cash cow* business has a product with a high market share and low but steady growth. Its organizational strategy is to maintain market share and use resources to fuel other activities of the organization such as question marks or rising stars.

- The *dog* has seen its market share diminish and growth potential curtailed. Its best probable organizational strategy is disinvestment or liquidation.

The BCG matrix can be a useful tool for a corporation that wants to better understand how its business units perform individually as well as contribute to the corporation as a whole. The matrix "facilitates corporate strategic analysis of likely 'generators' and optimum 'users' of corporate resources" (Pearce and Robinson, 1985, p. 242), as shown in Figure 3.

General Electric: The Planning Grid. General Electric (GE) and McKinsey and Co. took the BCG matrix a step further

Figure 3. BCG's Growth/Share Matrix.

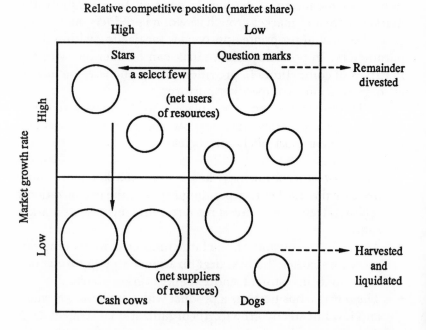

Source: Adapted from Barry Hedley, "Strategy and the Business Portfolio," *Long-Range Planning,* Feb. 1977, p. 10, as it appears in Pearce and Robinson, 1985, p. 243.

with their market attractiveness–business position matrix. Instead of four cells that run from high to low, the GE matrix introduces a medium range, resulting in a nine-cell planning grid (see Figure 4).

In addition, the GE approach relies on a number of factors, not just market share and market growth. For example, GE endorses using information about competitive status; customer and market knowledge; economic, social, and political conditions; and market growth rate as factors for determining market attractiveness. Information about channels of distribution, management and marketing expertise, and technology may be used to evaluate business position. GE leaves the inclusion or exclusion of factors on the matrix to the judgment of the organization's managers.

Use of the matrix is intended to guide managers toward one of three strategic approaches: (1) invest for growth, (2) invest selectively, or (3) divest (Abell and Hammond, 1979, pp. 212–220).

The Strategic Planning Institute: PIMS. PIMS, or the Profit Impact of Market Strategy, is a computer-based approach to strategy that was developed in the late 1960s.

The core of PIMS is a data base containing a minimum of four years of detailed operating and competitive data on each of more than twenty-eight hundred business units. These businesses cover a broad range of industries and markets from services to capital goods. The Strategic Planning Institute, a nonprofit organization of companies that have pooled their resources and experiences, houses the data base and administers the PIMS program. It provides its member companies with (1) access to the data base (under strict security provisions), (2) use of its proprietary computerized models, (3) PC software packages to aid management decision making, and (4) consulting services to its member companies.

Member companies supply the Strategic Planning Institute with data about their individual businesses, services, and products; revenues and costs; customers and primary competitors; assumptions about future sales; selling prices and raw

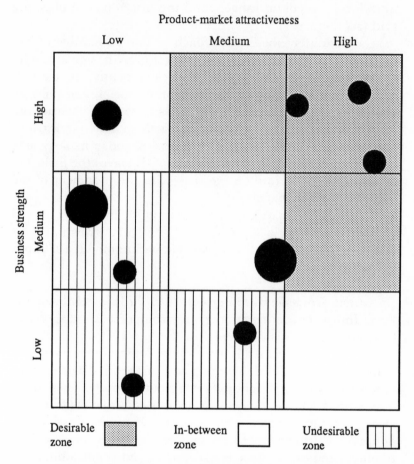

Figure 4. Market Attractiveness–
Business Position/Strength Matrix.

Source: Cravens, 1987, p. 80. Reprinted with permission of Richard D. Irwin, Inc., from *Strategic Marketing* (2nd ed.) by D. Cravens, copyright © 1987.

materials costs; and industry data. All such information is kept confidential. Through regression analysis PIMS attempts to discover relationships between business performance and variables such as technology, product life cycle stage, research and development investments, and patent protection.

PIMS research services include the preparation of reports

for management decision making. Such studies provide insights into such questions as:

- How will a change in strategy affect a business unit's financial performance?
- How can a business achieve gains in market share?
- What steps are needed to improve the quality of a product line (or service offering) relative to those of competitors?

The PIMS approach is based largely on the assertion that 67 percent of a business's performance is based on strategic factors such as investment intensity, productivity, market position, growth of the served market, quality of products or services, innovation and differentiation, vertical integration, cost push, and strategic effort (Cravens, 1987, p. 73).

Michael Porter: Five Competitive Forces. Michael Porter's *Competitive Strategy: Techniques for Analyzing Industries and Competitors* lays out an industry-specific strategic framework. It hinges on a thorough understanding of economic and technological forces influencing an organization's industry and competitors. Like the BCG and GE models, Porter's assumes that an organization's overarching questions concerning which markets to enter or exit have already been addressed and that strategic planning, including a thorough environmental scan, has occurred.

In Porter's view, "the rules of competition are embodied in five competitive forces: the entry of new competitors, the threat of substitutes, the bargaining power of buyers, the bargaining power of suppliers, and the rivalry among existing competitors. . . . The five forces determine industry profitability because they influence the prices, costs, and required investment of firms in an industry—the elements of return on investment" (Porter, 1985, pp. 4–5). These five forces are shown in Figure 5.

Porter's model requires that an organization have a broad understanding of its industry's structure, competitive dynamics, and evolutionary prospects. This contextual backdrop prepares the organization to (1) determine its relative position within the industry, (2) analyze the impact of the five competitive forces

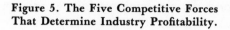

Figure 5. The Five Competitive Forces
That Determine Industry Profitability.

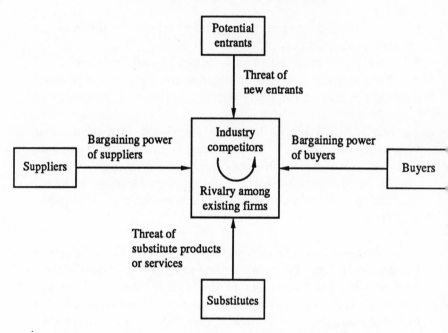

Source: Porter, 1985, p. 5. Reprinted with permission of the Free Press, a division of Macmillan, Inc., from *Competitive Advantage: Creating and Sustaining Superior Performance* by Michael E. Porter. Copyright © 1985 by Michael E. Porter.

on the firm, and (3) formulate strategies to gain competitive advantage.

Porter's approach to strategy formulation is an aggressive one that allows little room for the organization that is "holding the line." For him, the whole reason for setting strategy is to gain competitive advantage. His three "generic competitive strategies" for achieving above-average performance are:

- *cost leadership,* where a firm becomes the low-cost producer in its industry and takes whatever resource allocation steps that are necessary to sustain or enhance the cost advantage
- *differentiation,* where an organization scopes out and positions its product, service, or delivery system as "unique" in its industry, commanding premium prices

- *focus,* where an organization targets an industry segment or group of segments and tailors its strategy to serving them exclusively, establishing a cost advantage in its target segment (cost focus) or exploiting differences within the target segment (differentiation focus)

Miles and Snow: Strategic Patterns. In their 1978 book *Organizational Strategy, Structure, and Process,* R. E. Miles and C. C. Snow unveiled a model of corporate strategy that categorizes organizations according to their pattern of strategic decisions over time and asserts that these decisions represent predispositions to act in a certain way.

The categories of strategic behavior are:

- *defenders,* organizations that emphasize a narrow or limited product or service and engage in little or no product or market development, investing resources in the pursuit of efficiencies
- *prospectors,* organizations that constantly seek new opportunities, investing resources in pursuit of innovations and new market opportunities
- *analyzers,* organizations that exhibit characteristics of both defenders and prospectors and invest accordingly
- *reactors,* organizations that lack consistency, reacting to internal and external pressures with a patchwork quilt of strategic initiatives

John Pearce: Grand Strategies. Still another conceptual model takes a broad approach. Developed by John A. Pearce II, it is the centerpiece of *Strategic Management: Strategy Formulation and Implementation,* which Pearce first coauthored with Richard B. Robinson, Jr., in 1982. Pearce's model, largely based on concepts discussed in strategic literature for many years, asserts that there are twelve "grand" strategies that organizations use to be competitive: (1) concentration, (2) market development, (3) product development, (4) innovation, (5) horizontal integration, (6) vertical integration, (7) joint venture, (8) concentric diversification, (9) conglomerate diversification, (10) retrenchment/turnaround, (11) divestiture, and (12) liquidation.

These strategies provide the basic direction for a host of supporting strategic actions, including strategies at both the operational level (finance, marketing, manufacturing, and so on) and the corporate level (mergers, diversification, and so on). Sometimes referred to as master or business strategies, they are the basis for coordinated and sustained efforts directed toward achieving long-term business goals.

Any one of the grand strategies can serve as the basis for achieving the major long-term objectives of a single business. Some strategies are not usually pursued singly but rather in combination with one or more complementary strategies. For example, a joint venture strategy could easily accompany a strategy of market or product expansion. When a firm is involved in multiple businesses, industries, product lines, or customer groups — as many firms are — several grand strategies may be combined. Moreover, each strategic business unit or division has its own strategy under the large corporate strategy umbrella.

Pearce went on to cluster the strategies into four overarching categories:

- *Concentration,* when an organization focuses on doing what it does best within its established markets using essentially the same technology and marketing approach. The overarching strategy is to channel resources into existing efforts and "stick to your knitting."
- *Internal growth,* when an organization actively fosters innovation; expands its market; develops new, related products; or joins with another organization to strengthen its competitive position (joint venture). The overarching strategy is to channel resources toward building on existing strengths.
- *External growth (acquisition),* when an organization attempts to expand its resources or fortify its market position through the acquisition or creation of new businesses. An organization might move to acquire another organization that (1) is operating at the same level in the production-marketing chain (horizontal integration), (2) supplies the firm with materials or is a customer of the firm (vertical integration), (3) is unrelated to the organization's basic focus but might

enhance the acquiring firm's bottom line or tax position (concentric diversification), or (4) has good investment value and looks like a money-maker (concentric diversification). The overarching strategy is to channel existing resources toward the development of new resources.

* *Disinvestment,* when an organization is having economic and financial difficulties and moves to pare down its operations. The organization might move to cut costs or assets (retrenchment), redefine its goals (turnaround), sell off its parts (divestiture), or sell all its assets (liquidation). The overarching strategy is to minimize losses to the organization's stakeholders.

Adapting the Pearce model, we can take strategic thinking throughout an organization and recognize the impact of a particular grand strategy as it influences all the workings of the organization. This impact is felt as the operational units of the organization set their functional strategies designed to implement the grand strategies. Functional strategies include quality improvement, introduction and integration of new technology, transforming the organization through leadership, improving customer service, and downsizing. For example, in a grand "concentration strategy" the functional strategy of the production/operations/management division might be to improve quality so that the firm's product is seen as the best in its market.

Choosing a Framework

Although these models share the common intention of capturing the big picture, each has its own unique perspective. Perhaps the broadest and most comprehensive construct is that developed by Pearce. It not only incorporates many of the elements of the other constructs but also is flexible enough to accommodate cascading functional and tactical considerations such as training and development. Most importantly, its straightforward "snapshot" approach to understanding strategic overlays provides an opportunity for a structured analysis of training and development as part of the strategic picture, generating proactive thinking about human resource management in general and training in particular.

The following discussion, therefore, uses the Pearce framework as a basis for strategic discussions. However, this analysis adapts Pearce's cluster concept rather than adhering to Pearce's strict grand strategies approach. To simplify the discussion, we have elected to address Pearce's clusters as umbrella strategies and to explore and expand what Pearce calls "grand strategies" as areas of strategic emphasis (see Table 23).

Table 23. Umbrella Strategies and Their Strategic Emphases.

Umbrella Strategy	Strategic Emphasis
Concentration	Market share
	Operating costs
	Market niche
Internal growth	Market development
	Product development
	Innovation
	Joint venture
External growth	Horizontal integration
	Vertical integration
	Concentric diversification
Disinvestment	Retrenchment/turnaround
	Divestiture
	Liquidation

Within this framework, the analysis will explore the training and development implications of these umbrella strategies.

Thinking about organizational decisions against the backdrop of this conceptual model provides a global context in which to understand the circumstances that drive strategic choices (see Figure 6). This, in turn, enables the training and development advocate to easily use it to determine the training and development needs of his or her organization and to make cogent strategic arguments for investment by the organization.

Some Important Caveats. There are a few important things to remember when applying *any* strategic framework. The con-

Figure 6. Grand Strategy Selection Matrix.

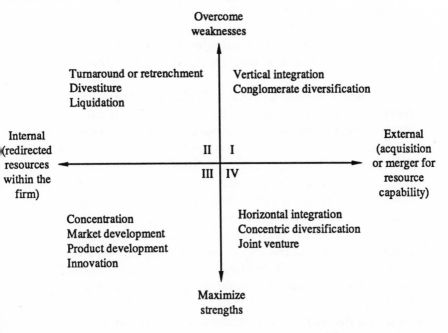

Source: Pearce and Robinson, 1985, p. 261. Reprinted with permission of Richard D. Irwin, Inc., from *Strategic Management: Strategic Formulation and Implementation* (2nd ed.) by J. A. Pearce II and R. B. Robinson, Jr., copyright © 1985.

ceptual model is a tool for understanding the strategic decision-making process. The actual process that a training and development advocate observes and seeks to influence in an organization will not be as clear-cut and precise as any model. Strategic choices are based on previous strategic choices and flow from them. They are not precise, nor are they sequential. Frequently, a combination of strategies may be employed.

The trick is to be able to understand the dynamics of the strategic planning and development process in an organization and to have a frame of reference that can help determine the likely implications of strategies as they are employed. The first rule of lobbying is intelligence. In order to influence, one needs to understand the whys and wherefores. Once a frame of reference is in place, the training and development advocate can move to influence the process, using some of the techniques outlined in Chapter Nine.

Umbrella Strategies and Their Training and Development Implications

Concentration: Courses of Action and Training Implications. When an organization considers adopting an umbrella strategy of concentration, it intends to stick to a single product or product line, focus on a current or familiar market, and use its existing technology. Concentration is usually low-risk, requires that few additional resources be invested, and, importantly, is based on the known competencies of the organization. Therefore, it is the most commonly employed strategy.

Perhaps more than any other strategy, concentration depends on the use of the organization's existing resources, both human and material. This places a premium on the current skills of the work force, and it demands that those skills be kept sharp. Under a strategy of concentration, an organization not only must maintain the quality of its human resources but also must develop those human resources.

The implication here is that the organization already has what it needs to develop and implement training, but those resources must be molded and organized so that they are more effectively and efficiently used. Training is likely to be designed, developed, and delivered internally and to focus mostly on developing existing resources so that they are fine-tuned and thus better suited for the single focus on a product, market, or technology.

There are several dynamic factors that influence the management of the work force under this strategy, and these factors have training implications. The internal environments of organizations — no matter how outwardly stable — experience change. Employees may be transferred or promoted; new employees may be hired. Orientation to new procedures, practices, and roles within the organization is important for both new hires and veteran employees who are attempting successful transitions to new jobs.

External factors sometimes intervene to influence the human resource agenda of an organization pursuing a concentration strategy. Regulatory changes can mean new training demands in areas such as safety or waste disposal. An organization may find its entry labor pool diminished due to wider opportunities caused by economic or labor market changes; forced to use less stringent hiring criteria, it may face training needs in areas such as basic reading, writing, or math skills.

Additional training needs will also result from the strategic emphasis that the organization selects in conjunction with the concentration strategy.

Early in the strategic planning process, planners begin to explore the various approaches and tactics that can be used within the parameters of a concentration strategy. In a stable market, an organization puts strategic emphasis on *increasing market share, reducing operating costs,* or *creating or maintaining a market niche.* The challenge of these three alternatives is that each places a different set of demands on the organization and its employee training and development efforts. The eventual success or failure of the strategy depends in part on how well the organization and its work force meet that challenge. Training and development issues may be critical across the board.

Increasing market share can be achieved by luring "repeat" customers away from the competition. Tactically, this can be achieved by improving the quality of the organization's product or service and constructing an advertising campaign that emphasizes this superior quality.

To realize success, the organization's employees must improve their performance at the point of production and point of sale. A heightened awareness of quality should pervade the firm's operations. This can be fostered through structural as well as cultural features of the organization, including quality circles, statistical quality control, and total quality assurance programs. The successful launching of such new initiatives hinges on specialized training and development programs.

Japanese companies have developed a number of interrelated practices for managing human resources in support of a strategic emphasis on quality. Lateral job rotation, dual promotion systems, work groups, consultative decision making, and the promise of job security are common in Japanese firms. Work groups are emphasized over individuals in the structure and assignment of tasks and in day-to-day problem solving. When performance is evaluated, individuals are measured for cooperation and interpersonal relations skills as well as technical competence.

One U.S. company that is operating under a concentration strategy, with a strategic emphasis on increasing market share, is Chemlawn, the North American leader in professional lawn care, headquartered in Columbus, Ohio. Like others in the lawn care industry, Chemlawn is experiencing a steadily declining customer base. Market analysis has shown that the decline is fueled by negative environmental publicity, perceptions of poor customer service, and concern about the price versus the value of the company's services given the wide array of available do-it-yourself products.

Chemlawn's approach to increasing market share hinges on addressing quality and price and value issues, discontinuing products that the public or environmental authorities perceive as unsafe, and improving the quality of its work force.

Customer service is a critical issue in this industry; frequently, good customer service is the critical difference that gives a company the edge over competitors. With this in mind, Chemlawn is using training and development as a tool to enhance its reputation in this arena. The key to this approach is linking the company's technical training system and customer service. Therefore, field service technician training now covers areas such as agronomies, safety, customer service, and interpersonal skills. Through this training Chemlawn emphasizes the direct relationship between customer satisfaction and employee motivations, loyalty, and professionalism.

Reducing operating costs can be achieved through productivity improvements or technological process innovations. The trick is to accomplish this without giving up anything in terms of the quantity and quality of output or the efficiency and effectiveness of operations. Possible tactics here include introducing new technology such as robots or computerized manufacturing systems or instituting the use of teams and removing artificial barriers to problem solving at the point of production or point of sale.

The use of these tactics can mean reductions in the work force, more decision making at the operational level, and changes in job classifications. Training would focus on integration of new technology, cross-training, interpersonal skills, and team building.

For example, Frito-Lay, a wholly owned subsidiary of Pepsico, Inc., headquartered in Plano, Texas, has undertaken an aggressive effort to concentrate on its core products and reduce its operating costs by improving productivity. As the largest snack food producer in the United States, the company has instituted the Frito-Lay Methods Improvement Program, which asks employees to suggest ways to increase productivity and improve product quality or the work environment.

Training plays a pivotal role in making this strategy a reality. Frito-Lay designs and develops technical training programs centrally, then delivers and evaluates the training on site. This saves costs because it avoids redundant design and development efforts while allowing training to be customized to meet individual plant needs. Moreover, it enables employees to receive a greater share of experiential training on the job. Actual training programs are geared toward meeting equipment operator job standards and mitigating quality, waste, and productivity problems that surface during training needs analysis and through examination of data compiled via computer-equipment interfaces in the production process.

Creating or maintaining a market niche can be a successful substrategy if the organization has some unique advantage relative to potential competitors and can protect its position in the niche. It can be accomplished by customizing products or services to meet the needs of special market segments or by engaging in "batch" processing, such as production in relatively small quantities of a product that is individually tailored to the customer.

Training and human resource development can be used to help the company protect its niche position. By taking measures that would be costly or difficult for competitors to imitate, a company can create mobility barriers that discourage others from entering the same market.

For example, custom and batch production requires different skills than does mass production. Custom production relies on the highly specialized skills of individual craftsmen. Operation of the programmable numerically controlled equipment used in batch production requires precision skills on the part of the operator in the areas of alignment, cleaning, speed adjustment, monitoring, and accident prevention. Programming skills are needed to reprogram the equipment, not to operate it. Engineering skills are necessary to design and set up an automated flexible manufacturing system for batch production (Blumenthal and Dray, 1985, pp. 30–37).

The organization can gain the competitive edge by investing in a highly specialized work force that is uniquely tailored to a particular task. On-the-job training may be used to encourage this specialization, whether it be in manufacturing, marketing, or another functional area.

ALCOA, the largest American and second-largest worldwide producer of aluminum and aluminum products, provides a good example of an organization utilizing a concentration strategy with a strategic emphasis on customization. Headquartered in Pittsburgh, Pennsylvania, ALCOA manufactures aluminum sheet for beverage cans, foil packaging, and closures for food products. It also supplies an array of aluminum products to the aerospace, automotive, and construction industries.

ALCOA's competitive edge is attained through customizing products that fill the exacting standards of its customers. To keep the company on top, ALCOA employees produce quality goods in a timely manner. This means they must strive for excellence in manufacturing, constantly measure performance, and minimize safety risks that could result in costly accidents and downtime.

Central training at ALCOA labs and at plant sites supports these goals. Central training has developed an extensive program in integrated manufacturing that incorporates all phases of product development from concept through customer service after the sale. In addition, apprentices and journeymen receive a tailored total quality control program at plant sites.

*Internal Growth: Courses of Action and Training Implica-
tions.* The umbrella strategy of internal expansion is relatively
low-risk and is rooted in the pursuit of gradual and steady growth
through emphasis on the organization's traditional strengths.
Strategic emphasis under this umbrella is likely to be on *market
development, product development, innovation,* and *joint ventures.*

A successful internal growth strategy depends greatly on
the management of the organization's human resources and the
careful application of training. Of course, as with any strategy,
the external environment may drive some training needs; regulatory changes and economic or labor market shifts may create
new training needs in areas such as safety and basic skills.
However, the organization that moves to use an internal expansion strategy has usually assessed the external environment
and made a conscious decision to reach beyond its existing
markets, products, or capabilities.

Equal care must be applied to understanding the internal environment of the organization and how it will be both
overtly and subtly affected by an internal growth strategy. Although internal growth strategies are characterized as "conser-
vative," they are marked by instability. Usual activities such
as hiring, transferring, and promoting take on unusual dimensions as an organization moves to expand. New facilities (plants
or offices), new equipment, and new manpower needs all present human resource management challenges.

Any organization employing an internal expansion strategy must address such issues. In addition, the choice of strategic
emphasis will have cascading implications for functional or
operational strategies and for employee training.

Strategic emphasis on market development means marketing existing products, making only superficial changes, to customers
in related market areas by adding channels of distribution or
changing advertising or promotional approaches.

While the pursuit of new markets may be sparked by the
decision makers of the organization, the successful penetration
of new markets depends on the ability of the marketing, sales,
and customer service work force to communicate product value.
Therefore, training in areas that support or promote high-quality
communications is key.

Of course, new employees must be trained thoroughly in areas such as product knowledge and the procedures and practices of the organization. However, new hands and old hands alike should be trained in interpersonal communications, negotiation, and thinking creatively about product applications.

Cheesebrough-Ponds, a major producer of health and beauty aids, elected several years ago to attempt to expand its market by repacking its Vaseline Petroleum Jelly in smaller, pocket-size squeeze tubes as Vaseline "Lip Therapy." The corporation made its decision to place a strategic emphasis on market development because it knew from market studies that its Petroleum Jelly customers were already using the product to prevent chapped lips. Company leaders reasoned that their market could be significantly expanded if the product were repackaged to conveniently fit in consumers' pockets or purses.

This decision had several training implications. New equipment for filling the small tubes was brought in, and machine operators were provided with training in setting up and operating the new equipment. This training was minimal, however, compared to the training for marketing and sales personnel responsible for moving the new product. Traditionally, petroleum jelly is sold on shelves inside the body of a store. But, for Lip Therapy to be a success, the company believed that it must be near store checkout counters with similar lip balm products. Sales personnel soon discovered that marketing at the checkout counter presented a different set of challenges from shelf marketing. As a result, the company spent approximately one and one-half years training its sales and marketing force in the fundamentals and principles of marketing at the checkout counter.

Moreover, if the organization decides to pursue new markets outside the United States, an additional set of considerations are likely to emerge. Development of foreign markets, often referred to as "global market expansion," has three dimensions: export, collaboration with foreign firms, and direct foreign investment. To pursue any or all of these, an organization often sends its own employees abroad, recruits U.S. citizens specifically for overseas assignments, or hires foreign nationals. Any of these actions creates a host of new situations and problems that demand training.

Success in overseas assignments depends on four sets of variables: (1) technical competence, (2) personality and interpersonal skills, (3) knowledge of the environment, and (4) personal and family situation (Tung, 1986, pp. 207–225).

Training programs enhance the employee's chances for success in an overseas assignment, given an acceptable level of technical skill. These include foreign language training, area studies, prior contact with members of the target foreign culture, and training in local customs and behavioral norms. Managers should also receive training on the cultural and legal implications of employing foreign nationals. As the difference between the United States and the target environment widens, training programs that prepare the employee and accompanying family members become more critical.

Interestingly, a recent study of overseas selection and training practices in eighty companies revealed that 68 percent of the firms did not have any type of training program for overseas assignments. When researchers looked at the reasons for failure to perform satisfactorily in an overseas assignment, they discovered a significant correlation between failure rates and selection and training practices (Tung, 1986, p. 220).

Depending on the length of the stay abroad and the extent of personal adjustment required, employees also face considerable readjustment when an assignment is over. Once back on home soil, the employee should be provided with reorientation and counseling.

Strategic emphasis on product development involves expanding an organization's product line by modifying existing products. Emphasis is usually on extending the life cycle of an existing product or on taking advantage of a favorable reputation or brand name. The purpose is to lead satisfied customers to new products as a result of a positive experience with the company's initial product.

Strategic emphasis on product development necessitates the development of an organizational culture that values change and fosters new ideas. It frequently means the introduction of

Exhibit 2. Internal Expansion: Looking at a Bank.

A financial institution with a strategy for internal growth may plan to open branch offices in neighboring communities or even add branches to communities that it currently serves. Given this strategy, some specific needs are likely to emerge. The organization needs tellers, bookkeepers, savings officers, loan officers, assistant managers, and managers to staff the new branches. On the day a branch office opens, these employees must have a full understanding of organization standards, policies, and procedures; know how to operate equipment (for example, on-line computer/teller system); and be adept at customer relations.

All employees at the new location will need to be integrated into the financial institution's system prior to the opening of the new branch. Tellers and savings personnel will usually be put through a formal internal training program (usually an ongoing, existing training program of one to three weeks in duration) and then sent to a branch for on-the-job training and integration. Lending and managerial personnel may also go through a formal training program, which usually extends beyond a few weeks and also involves a great deal of informal on-the-job training.

In addition to training on organization policies and procedures, new employees will need training for product knowledge and for the ability to sell and cross-sell. While these abilities are necessary in existing branches, they may be critical to the success of a new branch location.

Location also drives some training decisions. Moving into a new governmental jurisdiction requires understanding the local laws and regulations as they affect the business.

In addition, the customer base may be significantly different from the one that the bank traditionally serves. Customer service training begins with knowing the demographics of the new location, including the needs of your customers and their ability to understand and purchase your services. Unique challenges can be presented by the population's language, culture, socioeconomic status, or median age.

---

new technology, practices, and distribution systems. It requires employees who understand the organization's products and their capabilities and limitations, are creative but have a practical bent, are flexible and adaptable, and can be somewhat evangelistic in pursuing "the new and improved" and identifying or creating markets for the new product(s).

Training and development play a critical two-tiered role for the organization pursuing product development. On the one tier is training that assists in the development of an organizational culture that values creative thinking throughout—not just at the top levels of management, and particularly at the point of production or sale of existing products. Quality circles or other informal forums where employees gather and exchange ideas should be fostered and accompanied by training that builds strong group interaction such as in team building, communications (both listening and speaking), conflict resolution, and interpersonal skills.

On the other tier is training that assists employees to achieve technical competence in their jobs. The development of new products often means the introduction of new machines, practices, or procedures. Training to assist new and veteran employees to achieve proficiency in product knowledge, new equipment operations, or new sales and marketing strategies is essential to success.

Nabisco Brands, Inc., seeks competitive advantage by placing its strategic emphasis on product development. Headquartered in Parsippany, New Jersey, the company is one of three operating units of RJR Nabisco. It is the leading producer of biscuits, confections, snacks, shredded cereals, and processed fruit and vegetables. To maintain its position as leader, Nabisco pursues a strategy of developing and introducing new products and expanding its existing product line. Spoon Size Shredded Wheat and Ritz Bits crackers are two examples of new products that are variations on existing products.

Success in this arena requires substantial investment in manufacturing, processing, and packaging technology. These investments can only be put to maximum use if the work force can operate and maintain equipment cost-effectively. To ensure this, Nabisco training staff members attend demonstrations of new equipment that Nabisco is considering for purchase. The training implications of the purchase are considered, and, once the buy is set, training staff works with the original equipment manufacturers (OEMs) and plant operations personnel to design training and deliver it at plant sites.

The McDonald's restaurant chain also employs an internal growth strategy that places strategic emphasis on product development. Originally, McDonald's marketed a limited product line centering on hamburgers, french fries, and soft drinks. But within the last decade the "golden arches" have expanded to include a wide selection of breakfast foods and have expanded their core menu to include everything from salads to chicken. Training in the preparation of the new products, as well as interpersonal skills to prepare employees to provide customers with information on new products, is essential and ongoing. A thorough orientation to the new products and what they mean to the way the company and its employees are viewed by customers is essential.

Strategic emphasis on innovation shifts an organization's focus toward creating new or different products. In the competitive arena, innovations are divided into two categories: incremental and radical.

Incremental innovation is embedded in product development, where the emphasis is on creating new variations of existing products. Its focus is on extending and amplifying the life cycle of existing products.

Radical innovation is the pursuit of major breakthroughs that represent a new standard in products or practices. It starts a new product life cycle that makes any similar product obsolete.

Strategic emphasis on innovation is not confined to new products or new product technologies, however. Some organizations pursue innovation in their organizational arrangements as well as in areas such as marketing, advertising, sales, and distribution.

Innovation is characterized by wide-ranging exploration as manufacturers test diverse product concepts in the market. To succeed in this type of environment, a firm must be both highly sensitive to the market and very flexible in responding to a product concept that is still taking shape in the mind of the consumer. Moreover, the organization must recognize that rapid innovation entails simultaneous development of design, production, and marketing aspects of a product. The organization must be willing to modify established practices or even to waive them.

Communication is key. Without it, top management risks becoming isolated from its own production system because it is new and unfamiliar. From the perspective of those who are trying to innovate, bureaucratic requirements for documentation, approval, funding, and so on can increase frustration levels and waste time. Conventional incentives may discourage the exploratory, risk-taking behavior that is essential to some types of innovation (Quinn, 1985, pp. 73–84).

Companies have devised a variety of solutions to this problem. One is to set up a special project team to manage the new venture, with representatives from R&D, production, marketing, and finance, headed by an entrepreneurial leader (Betz, 1987). Another is to provide a semiautonomous structure within the larger organizational framework with separate funding and a mandate to chart its own course in pursuit of given strategic objectives. If the fit between this entrepreneurial unit and the parent firm is smooth, such an arrangement can cultivate a subenvironment that is favorable to innovation within the constraints of a more traditional bureaucratic organization. Training and development are useful to gain acceptance for the innovative unit.

Since the cost of research, development, and premarketing is high but necessary to convert a promising idea into a profitable product, few radically innovative ideas prove to be truly profitable. Consequently, few organizations invest large resources in fostering radical innovation as their primary way of relating to their markets. However, when organizations do search for and attempt a novel idea, there are training and development implications to consider.

Creative thinking and analytical skills are essential to innovation. An organization utilizing an innovation strategy should attempt to cultivate a work force that has these skills from the line to the boardroom, not just in the research department. For example, training employees to participate in quality circles has had some success, resulting in both incremental and radical product innovations.

Moreover, managers and supervisors must play a pivotal role in creating a "safe" environment for risk taking. They must understand how to "grow" employees who are self-starters, encouraging and balancing employee ideas in a nonjudgmental and motivating fashion. Therefore, feedback and communications skills are essential.

Supervisory training should include providing an awareness that the nurturing of high performance is an ongoing process requiring regular, informal feedback and that formal performance evaluations are summarizations of an ongoing process. Critical to this awareness is training in techniques for delivering both positive and negative feedback that motivates employees to perform. Last, supervisors need training to enhance their knowledge about group dynamics (research has shown that groups tend to make riskier decisions than do individuals) and about how to develop checks and balances that keep the creative process on a realistic track.

Actually producing a new and innovative product also poses a number of training challenges. New manufacturing processes require new expertise. Old facilities might need to be transformed, or new facilities might need to be opened. In either case, workers need to be hired, oriented, and trained. After the product is manufactured, it must be advertised and sold. Sales and staff employees will need to be educated about the product's uses, advantages, and disadvantages and, importantly, why customers should go with the new over the old "tried and true."

INTEL, a designer and manufacturer of semiconductor components and related computers, microcomputer systems, and software for OEMs, pursues expansion through a strategic emphasis on innovation. Headquartered in California, the company has continually been a leader in the semiconductor industry; it is currently working on a microprocessor that is expected to revolutionize the PC industry by giving a desktop computer the capability of today's mainframe.

INTEL uses a strict screening process to select and place new employees. Extensive technical training is provided for both new hires and experienced employees. Employees also receive training designed to encourage creativity and to promote greater awareness of new product and manufacturing technology.

In addition, the training and development department itself is charged with playing a key role in pursuing innovation. The staff is trained to continually search, through close observation and involvement, for barriers to efficient achievement of the company's strategic goals at the plant sites. Challenges are discussed with management, and training is often used as a tool to foster creative thinking and develop innovative ideas.

Strategic emphasis on joint venture, where two companies seek to gain a competitive edge by pursuing expansion through joint ownership, is increasingly common. Through joint venture, an organization supplements its traditional strengths with the strengths of a companion organization.

The coming together of two separate organizations with their separate cultures and styles can create a number of challenges. Mitigating factors include the degree of interaction between the two organizations' employees and the level or levels of interaction (top management only, line workers to line workers, and so on).

Employees may need to be trained in effective inter- and intraorganization conflict, participative decision making, effective collaboration, negotiation, and other related behavioral areas. In addition, a need for technical proficiency in the companion organization's technology, practices, or procedures may drive training.

Another twist on the joint venture story comes when domestic firms join foreign businesses through joint ownership. Some countries, such as India and Mexico, mandate that foreign companies entering their markets do so on the basis of joint ownership. These countries believe that joint ventures minimize the threat of foreign domination and enhance the skills, employment, growth, and profits of local businesses. This creates a set of training needs similar to those discussed in the section on market development in foreign countries.

Diamond-Star Motors is the result of a joint venture between a U.S. company, Chrysler Corporation, and Japan's Mitsubishi Motors Corporation. Located in Normal, Illinois, Diamond-Star was launched because it offered the opportunity for Chrysler and Mitsubishi to expand on their long-standing relationship in which subcompact cars (as well as Mitsubishi engines and other automotive parts) are imported to the United States and sold under the Dodge and Plymouth name plates.

The joint venture extends that supplier-consumer relationship and has strategic advantages for both partners. For

Chrysler it presents an opportunity to produce a high-quality car using expertise brought to the venture by Mitsubishi and the chance to try new production techniques and realize efficiencies by using a work force that was not included under Chrysler's collective bargaining agreement with the United Auto Workers (UAW). For Mitsubishi it offers the opportunity to produce cars for sale in the United States without being subjected to the import tariffs and restrictions placed on Japanese imports. For both the venture presents an opportunity to mitigate the high cost of plant start-up and operation.

Diamond-Star is managed according to the principles of Japanese management. Under this approach, employees are expected to be more flexible and dedicated, and they are encouraged to make more suggestions than are workers on typical U.S. automotive production lines. New job applicants must take a battery of written tests as well as a physical examination and drug test. After passing, applicants begin extensive training that includes not only basic-level job training but team-building and interpersonal skills training as well. This prehire training eliminates about 40 percent of those applicants who pass initial screening (Hampton, 1988).

After being hired, Diamond-Star employees begin extensive training ranging from basic job training to kaizen (continuous line technological innovation). This training is then followed by several weeks of job-specific technical training, then several more weeks of supervised on-the-job training.

American workers must prove that they can adapt to an organizational culture that is distinctly Japanese. The training department bears lead responsibility for integrating workers into this culture and ensuring that employees embrace the Japanese management style that the company feels is essential to its success. Its mission is to ensure that employees understand and participate in the organizational culture. The training staff itself must absorb and embrace the Japanese culture and management style to such a degree that they can motivate employees to embrace it. Therefore, they embed the principles of kaizen, team building, and interpersonal skills in all phases of technical training.

External Growth (Acquisition): Courses of Action and Training Implications. Organizations attempting to expand through acquisition of other organizations or businesses are operating under the umbrella strategy of external growth. Strategic emphasis is usually placed on acquisition in order to integrate new resources or diversify holdings.

Integration is pursued in two ways:

- *Horizontal integration,* when an organization acquires a business or businesses operating at the same stage in the production-marketing chain, providing access to new markets for the acquirer and eliminating competitors.
- *Vertical integration,* when an organization acquires one or more businesses that can supply the acquirer or buy its products, providing opportunities for cost control and increased profits.

Diversification also has two routes:

- *Concentric diversification,* when an organization acquires new businesses that are compatible with the acquiring organization because they have similar markets, products, or technologies, providing opportunities to better balance profit and losses or to diversify a product line.
- *Conglomerate diversification,* when an organization acquires other businesses that have nothing in common with the acquiring organization. Acquisition is based solely on the organization's ability to increase profit or offset tax losses.

When exploring the training and human resource management implications of an umbrella strategy of external growth, one thing immediately becomes clear. When the strategic emphasis is on conglomerate diversification, the organization does not intend to integrate the diverse work forces. The training implications, therefore, are minimal, if any, and would focus entirely on educating top managers in the corporation about the newly acquired entities.

The other three approaches—horizontal integration, vertical integration, and concentric diversification—give rise to managerial problems and organizational issues associated with assimilating separate entities into an integrated whole. They also share a common set of training and development issues that are the focus of the following discussion.

Unlike internal expansion strategies, which are characterized by the creation of new jobs and tasks to accommodate growth, external acquisition strategies frequently are marked by restructuring and layoffs. Thus, when an organization bases its plans for expansion on acquiring existing businesses, through either integration or diversification, the result is likely to be a period of uncertainty or even chaos.

Acquisition strategies create a whole set of issues involving the cultural dynamics of both the acquiring and the acquired organizations, including integration of organizational cultures; integration of organizational structures, possibly leading to layoffs of employees at all levels; and increased complexity of top management tasks such as leadership, coordination, and control.

The morale and enthusiasm of a work force frequently suffer after an organization is acquired. Employees grapple with a period of uncertainty, often exacerbated by the departure of key managers. Employees experience difficulty maintaining a uniform level of performance and commitment as the organization changes around them. The unavailability of reliable information during the transitional period, especially questions concerning the nature and magnitude of the changes taking place, may foster frustration and decrease productivity.

While fear of losing one's job is perhaps the most obvious source of anxiety in a newly acquired firm, uncertainty regarding changes in the job itself (including roles, responsibilities, and location), rewards (salary, benefits, and perks), career paths, political relationships, co-workers, and corporate culture may also come into play (Schweiger, Ivancevich, and Power, 1987, p. 123).

Moreover, when the strategic emphasis is placed on merging two organizations, culture clash almost certainly results. This is true even for organizations within the same industry, as in the case of horizontal integration, because culture is unique to each individual firm. The problem increases with the degree of disparity between the two cultures and with the level of unification that needs to be achieved.

If the acquiring and acquired firms differ significantly in terms of mission, values, behavioral norms, and belief systems, attempting to integrate them causes organizational members to suffer a certain degree of culture shock. If the disparity is too great, it contributes to miscommunication, misinterpretation, and a general lack of trust among members of the two organizational cultures.

It is essential that the skills and abilities of each organization's work force as well as its attitudes, values, and beliefs be determined. As they are integrated, redundancy between the work forces may crop up; that is, more talent than is actually needed may be present. Attitudes toward the merger/acquisition may cause problems (including job insecurity, dissatisfaction, and animosity) rather than help the transition. Consequently, training might need to focus more on attitudes and processes than on specific skills.

Since most employees interact with the organization through their immediate supervisor, programs that train supervisors to handle sensitive situations, listen, and communicate effectively can make a great difference in how situations are perceived and in how well they are accepted by those remaining in the organization.

Norfolk Southern Corporation, a rail and road transportation company headquartered in Norfolk, Virginia, faced the challenges of external growth. Among its wholly owned subsidiaries are Southern Railway, Norfolk & Western Railway, and North American Van Lines. Since the merger of the Norfolk & Western and Southern Railway systems, Norfolk Southern has been heavily involved in consolidating its transportation departments and in restructuring operations.

Virtually every employee of both systems required some type of training in the methods and procedures of the combined rail operations or in operation of new or unfamiliar equipment. In addition, extensive training in team building at all levels and throughout all functions of the corporation was seen as essential to mitigating potential problems.

The training was developed by Southern Railway's training department. Since they were retraining many former Norfolk & Western employees, they were particularly aware of personal sensitivities as well as training for learning transfer to new systems.

More than under any other strategy, external growth (acquisition) holds the possibility that the training and development function itself may be reorganized because it is redundant. Existing training and development programs may be so specialized or tailored that they are not transferable or usable in the new atmosphere of the merger. They may overlap with programs offered by the acquiring organization in content or intent. However, programs or content areas can be modified to offer employees the best of both worlds and to expand employee development opportunities.

A merger causes those staffing the training function to confront many of the same issues with which other employees must deal — loss of job, culture shock, and shifting priorities. Training to assist the trainers in dealing with these pressures is an important step toward building a training "transition team" that moves work forces together.

For example, at Norfolk Southern Corporation the merger resulted in the elimination of Norfolk & Western's training department. All training personnel were provided orientation concerning Southern Railway's training philosophy and programs. Those who wanted to stay in training were able to do so by being absorbed into Southern's training department. The remaining trainers were subject matter experts or operations people who elected to be reabsorbed into operations or who chose early retirement.

Disinvestment: Courses of Action and Training Implications. An organization may be compelled to shift into a strategy of disinvestment when it becomes overextended in a given market, it suffers economic reversals because of competitive or other environmental pressures, customer demand for its products or services declines, or its resources are redirected by the organization's stakeholders to more attractive strategic alternatives. Once this strategy is selected, the organization may elect to pursue it by placing strategic emphasis on *retrenchment, turnaround, divestiture,* or *liquidation.*

Unlike the previous strategies of concentration, internal growth, and external growth (acquisition), the notion of disinvestment suggests that the firm is having economic and financial difficulties and must pare down its operations accordingly. For obvious reasons, this emphasis on cost reduction is likely to result in a paradox for training: the organization is reluctant to invest new money in training, even though training might ultimately result in cost reductions. In a sense, therefore, it is harder to make a case for the value of training in organizations faced with disinvestment. However, there are training possibilities and opportunities for employees whose companies are disinvesting.

Strategic emphasis on retrenchment is applied when organizational leaders, faced with economic reversals and declining profits, believe that the organization can survive only through returning to its basic strengths.

The battle cry of the organization emphasizing retrenchment is to do more with less. Then, if the organization can hold on and improve its position, it can shift its strategic emphasis and its resources toward turning the organization around.

Three approaches are commonly employed under retrenchment: cost reduction, asset reduction, and revenue generation. Cost reductions may be realized by extending the life of existing machinery or by cutting back on the work force. Asset reductions are achieved whenever land, buildings, equipment, and the like are sold off. Revenue generation efforts (absent increased sales) often focus on improving inventory controls and streamlining bill collection procedures.

These approaches imply that the organization must use its human and other resources more efficiently than in the past. Accomplishing this requires some structural adjustment to introduce and institutionalize new work-related values and to get the organization moving on an upward curve.

Administrative and operating procedures can be streamlined to increase efficiency without sacrificing quality or effectiveness. Tasks and responsibilities may have to be reallocated as job slots are recombined and managerial layers are eliminated.

Training that focuses on the shifting organizational culture can assist greatly in this effort. Training should include motivation and goal setting, time management, stress management, and cross-training in multiple skills. Pragmatism and action orientation should be the overriding concern of any training program under a retrenchment strategy. If layoffs have occurred, outplacement needs (for example, training for interviewing and resume writing) often arise.

Ford Motor Company, a major manufacturer of automobiles, trucks, farm implements, aerospace systems, communications equipment, and electronic systems, pursued a strategy of retrenchment in the late 1970s and early 1980s. After several years of declining market share and profits, the company elected to reorganize and lay the groundwork for recovery. Ford hoped that the steps it envisioned as part of retrenchment would strengthen the company enough to launch a turnaround strategy. First, Ford moved to cut costs by reducing employment by 143,000 workers, or 28 percent of the work force. At the same time, however, it increased training and development for its remaining workers, focusing on cross-training and retraining for line workers as well as on team building for all employees.

Strategic emphasis on turnaround is applied if retrenchment efforts succeed; an organization's next step is to redefine itself and its goals. When the strategic emphasis shifts to turnaround, the organization is in a state of transition and requires thoughtful reallocation of resources toward the new strategic goal of profitability.

Interestingly, the resource most commonly reallocated in the implementation of a turnaround strategy is management talent. Organizations that have their strategic sights set on a turnaround frequently believe that success can be achieved by bringing on a fresh managerial perspective. They attempt to motivate employees to adopt change through the inspired leadership of a new executive player. This can be very effective in raising employee morale and keeping employees involved in the success of the organization.

The issue of maintaining employee morale is not a small one for an organization in transition. Morale affects performance on the job. Performance in the face of often severe resource limitations can mean the difference between turnaround and failure.

By shifting the way that the work force interacts with management, an organization can make significant strides toward the transformation from loser to winner. Reducing or eliminating organizational barriers, instituting participative management, encouraging open communications, and increasing decision making and autonomy at the point of production or point of sale can make a difference.

Training is key to all of these approaches. It is a tool to get managers and other employees to rethink their assumptions and arrive at new understandings. Managers should receive leadership training, since leadership is crucial in formulating and articulating the shared vision that lies at the heart of directed change. Organizational design must be modified, both to uncouple outmoded patterns of behavior from their support structure and to give strength and substance to the new behaviors that must be adopted if the transformation is to succeed. Training in areas such as new policies, procedures and practices, goal setting and motivation, and interpersonal communication should be supplied for all employees.

For example, even as Ford Motor Company instituted its retrenchment strategy, it was positioning itself to shift into a turnaround strategy. Ford began to espouse a new philosophy that emphasized employees' working as a team toward the common goals of producing the highest-quality products of their kind in the world. Training and development were assigned a major tactical role in the turnaround, supporting both the cultural and the technological changes that Ford needed for success. To underpin the cultural shift, both salaried and hourly workers were provided opportunities to learn how to work together more efficiently, how to be more focused and more productive, and how to make suggestions to their supervisors. Training also facilitated the integration of new equipment such as robots and new processes such as statistical quality control.

Strategic emphasis on divestiture or liquidation occurs when retrenchment fails to trigger the desired turnaround and organizational leaders move toward these strategies of last resort.

The theory behind a divestiture strategy is that by selling off the parts, the core or parent organization can be made stronger and survive. For large corporations, this may mean selling off whole businesses. For smaller enterprises, it may mean selling off parts of the business.

The adoption of a liquidation strategy signals the end of an organization. The strategy focuses on selling off all tangible assets in order to realize the greatest possible return on investment for the stakeholders of the organization.

Training and development considerations under divestiture and liquidation strategies are few. Appropriate alternatives include outplacement for displaced employees and training in stress management. Outplacement assistance includes office space, telephones, administrative assistance, job search advice, and counseling. Job search skills training might include how to conduct a skills inventory, resume preparation, interviewing skills, communication skills, and negotiation. If early retirement is encouraged, programs might focus on illustrating the benefits of retirement and skills to make the transition from work to retirement a success.

Realistically, however, most firms faced with the admission of failure that triggers divestiture or liquidation are in no position to underwrite such training. When assistance is provided, it is often through the voluntary efforts of individual trainers whose own work load is diminishing as a result of cutbacks and who play the role of outplacement counselor on a sporadic basis.

If a firm is willing and able to provide formal outplacement assistance, it could take a lesson from Crouse-Hinds/ Cooper Industries (Crouse), a manufacturer of electrical construction materials. Although Crouse was not divesting or liquidating itself, it was going through a period of downsizing in the mid 1980s. Buffeted by shifts in the economy, Crouse determined that it had to lay off a number of workers.

Crouse decided to offer an outplacement program for workers targeted for layoffs. Its goal was to provide job training and placement assistance in a positive environment. Before announcing the layoffs, Crouse set about researching available resources for displaced workers and:

- identified a state program to provide $1,500 to each affected employee for retraining
- identified the types of training that would be beneficial to the affected employees and made arrangements for the training to be provided
- established a program to provide training in resume writing and interviewing skills as well as computer use
- arranged for off-site facilities to provide typing support, telephone use, and a library for the personnel

When layoffs were announced (on a Friday), all employees were invited to attend the first outplacement session the following Monday. By scheduling the session so quickly after layoffs, Crouse hoped to increase participation in the outplacement program as well as to mitigate morale problems that the laid-off workers would have. All laid-off workers attended the meeting, which was designed to explain the services that would be available to personnel as well as to show that no one was in isolation and that by talking and exchanging ideas, the laid-off workers could serve as an informal support group for each other.

As a result of the program, 45 percent of the employees were placed within eight to ten weeks after layoff. All personnel were placed within six months.

CHAPTER 8

Gathering Strategic Information: Questions to Ask

The first step toward influencing the strategic decision-making process and driving training considerations throughout that process is intelligence gathering. As soon as the training and development advocate knows that his or her organization is considering employing a strategy, he or she needs information in order to contribute to the success of that strategy. The organization's planners should be able to provide answers to broad questions, while the advocate may need to discover and develop responses to human resource questions.

Following are some questions to guide training professionals in their efforts to gather information and begin participating in the strategic process. They are organized into two broad groupings: (1) common considerations, or those relevant regardless of the strategy employed, and (2) specific considerations, or those that are essential for each type of strategy employed.

Keep in mind that these questions — while designed to help develop a comprehensive picture — may only begin the journey into the strategic jungle. Unique organization circumstances can always lead to further questions.

Common Considerations

The answers to the following questions will be important regardless of the strategy:

Broad Issues

- The training advocate needs to understand the environment in which her or his organization operates. Is the organization's current industry evolving or stable? What do the growth trends in the industry look like? Who are the main domestic and foreign competitors, and what is the organization's competitive advantage over those competitors? How can or will the organization capitalize on competitors' strategic vulnerabilities? (For example, is the organization capable of widening the competitive gap in its favor?)

- Why has the organization been successful in the past? What strategies has it successfully employed? What was learned during that time that can be applied under the new strategy? What forces have driven the organization to select a new strategy?

- What technology does the organization plan to use? If the organization plans to use new technology, when will it come on line? Any new processes? When will they be instituted?

- Are innovations anticipated in the industry that could change the competitive playing field? Will these be radical breakthroughs or modifications to existing products or technologies? What effect would this have on the organization's product and its competitive position?

- What new management philosophies or procedures such as constant quality pursuit (kaizen), working through teams, and participative management will be instituted by the organization? When?

- Are there any regulatory issues — current, pending, or anticipated — that could influence strategic considerations?

- What functional strategies will be employed by the various divisions or operating units to effect the overarching strategy? Why? How?

Human Resource Issues

- The training advocate needs to understand the workplace profile of the organization. What are the current strengths and weaknesses of the work force? In the aggregate, is the work force technical? Is it skilled? What kind of education or training have most employees received to enter their positions? What do they need to stay current? Is it a flexible and adaptable work force?

- What changes, if any, must occur in the job(s), organizational culture, and skill levels of the work force?
- Is the organization's decision to pursue an umbrella strategy likely to result in layoffs or other turnover? How much is anticipated?
- How will union contract agreements be affected? What is the strategic role of the union?
- What human resource management policies should be reviewed or modified in light of the organization's strategic emphasis (such as selection, hiring, appraisal, rewards, or career development)?
- What are the training implications of the overarching strategy? Of each functional/operational strategy and its companion tactics? How could training help the organization reach any or all of its strategic goals?
- What kind of specific training programs are needed? Are they needed in basic workplace, technical, product knowledge, managerial/supervisory, or motivational skills? Does the organization have in-house capability to implement the necessary programs? Are there outside experts who can assist? Who are they?
- How has training been regarded by the work force in the past? By management? How credible are the programs and the trainers? How will these views affect future training efforts?
- What delivery mechanisms are most cost-effective and practical for each training program?
- Does the organization have an employee educational assistance plan (tuition reimbursement)? Do many employees take advantage of it? If so, how can it be used to enhance worker skills?
- What kind of training evaluation process is currently being used? Does it provide information on return on investment

(ROI)? If not, would such a process contribute to the strategic information flow?

- Is there a formal procedure to ascertain if current training is appropriate in light of a new strategy or, alternatively, to identify training needs that will be dictated by the new strategy?
- Do human resource management functions other than training (such as selection, hiring, appraisal, rewards, or career development) need to be reviewed? Should they be modified?

Considerations Specific to Each Strategy

These questions are meant to supplement the common considerations listed above. They attempt to address some of the subtleties of each umbrella strategy.

Concentration Strategy

Strategy focus includes sticking to a single product, in a single market, using a single technology. Strategic emphasis options include increasing market share, reducing operating costs, or creating or maintaining a market niche.

- Which strategic emphasis option(s) will the organization choose? Why?
- Recognizing that a concentration strategy demands that work-force skills be kept sharp, what systematic approach will be taken to maintain and develop the organization's human capital?
- What structural and cultural innovations, such as quality circles, statistical quality control, or total quality assurance, could be introduced to heighten the organization's awareness of quality?

Internal Growth Strategy

Strategy focus includes pursuing gradual and steady growth through emphasis on the organization's traditional strengths.

Strategic emphasis options include market development, product development, innovation, or joint ventures.

- What market factors make the organization believe it can expand to increase its competitive advantage?
- How rapidly and extensively does the organization want to grow?
- Where will the organization place strategic emphasis? (For example, how does the organization plan to grow?) Through market development? Product development? Innovation? Joint venture? A combination of two or more?
- What is the organization's projected growth time line?
- Does the organization plan to open new facilities or operations? How many? Where? Over what time period? How many new employees will be needed?
- Does the organization plan to try to attract a new or expanded customer base? Will this require hiring more employees?
- What new products will be introduced? Over what time period? Will new equipment be needed to produce the new products?
- How often will new products be brought on line or introduced? Will there be a continual stream of new and different products to be made, sold, or marketed?

When the Strategic Emphasis Is on Market Development

- Will the organization need to add to its existing work force? Are suitable workers available in your geographical area? What is the forecast regarding supply and demand?
- Will current employees be asked to take on new responsibilities or tasks?
- Is the training function equipped to handle the integration of a wave of new employees?
- Will subject matter experts need to be identified and trained to assist in the training effort? What are the train-the-trainer considerations?
- If physical market expansion such as the construction or purchase of new facilities is planned, are training and develop-

ment staff involved in those discussions to offer insights? Will training and development be on site as new facilities are opened or centralized?

- Since the sales force is pivotal in this area, what qualifications must new hires have? How will the sales force get trained and retrained?
- If foreign expansion is planned, what are the training and development implications? What and who are the resources for this? Are in-house trainers equipped to handle these changes? To make informed decisions about the purchase of training dealing with these issues?

When the Strategic Emphasis Is on Product Development

- What are the technological implications of product development? Marketing implications? Distribution implications?
- How will technical training be provided? Will OEMs assist?
- What will be done to create an atmosphere that nurtures product improvements and spin-offs (referred to as incremental innovation)?
- Are new products intended to fill a niche or to break new ground? If they are breaking new ground, how will the organization prepare its sales force to get its customers to realize they need the new product?
- What training is needed? Can it be provided with in-house resources, or are outside providers needed?
- Will subject matter experts need to be identified and trained to assist in the training effort? What are the train-the-trainer considerations such as time and cost?

When the Strategic Emphasis Is on Innovation

- What existing policies or practices need to be modified or eliminated in order to promote innovative thinking?
- Are there specific resources set aside for R&D? How does R&D staff interact with line managers? Line workers?
- Does the organization create an atmosphere that encourages all employees to think innovatively? Is this a "safe" environment? Is risk taking encouraged? How do supervisors pro-

vide feedback? How do they help employees balance ideas? Are employees rewarded for their innovations?

- How does management first react to the new and unfamiliar? How do they differentiate between practical ideas and off-the-wall ideas? Is training needed here?
- If an entrepreneurial unit approach is used, how is the remaining work force encouraged to view that team? Is the team accessible? How does it relate to the R&D unit?
- Does the training and development department function as an observer, reactor, or catalyst to innovation? What is the feedback loop?

When the Strategic Emphasis Is on Joint Venture

- Are the cultures and philosophies of the joining organizations similar? If not, which organizational philosophy will prevail? What challenges are anticipated as a result of such integration?
- Do the organizations have similar perspectives on training and human resource management and development? If not, how will the two perspectives be integrated?
- If employees from the existing work forces are used, what cultural differences might emerge that could have an impact?
- With what additional problems — other than those typically associated with new start-ups — will human resource development professionals need to contend?
- Who will be responsible for orientation and training? One or both of the partners?
- If, as in the case of Chrysler and Mitsubishi, a foreign culture must be integrated, are in-house trainers equipped to facilitate the integration? Can they make informed decisions about the purchase of outside training resources to deal with these issues?
- What is the nature of the organization's orientation to training and development and human resource management?

External Growth Strategy

Strategy focus is to expand through acquisition of other organizations. Strategic emphasis options include securing new holdings in order to integrate new resources with existing capabilities or diversifying holdings.

- How might the organization's acquisition plans change its industry profile?
- How will the organization's competitive advantage be enhanced through the planned acquisition(s)?
- How rapidly and extensively does the organization want to grow?

When the Strategic Emphasis Is on Integration

- Does the organization plan to buy up others in the same industry or business?
- Does the organization plan to buy a peripherally related business? Does the acquired organization impact the acquiring organization's inputs or outputs? More specifically, is it a supplier to or consumer of the acquiring organization's products?
- What is the acquired organization's competitive advantage? Why was it selected for acquisition? How will it enhance the acquiring organization? What are its mission and goals? Its competitive strategies and tactics?
- Does the acquired organization use different production technologies or processes? What kind of facilities and equipment does the acquired organization have? How will these be integrated with the acquiring organization's?
- What does the culture of the other organization look like? What are the behavioral norms and the belief systems? Are these similar to those of the acquiring organization? How are they different? What challenges does this present for the acquiring organization?
- How far apart are the two organizations geographically? How will this affect integration efforts? Are there cultural considerations?
- What are the age differences of the organizations? Are they at roughly the same stage in their organizational life cycles? How far apart are they? Will this help or hinder integration efforts?

- Are the organizations roughly the same size? If not, how different are they, and what will this mean to integration efforts?
- Are the organizations structured the same? If differently, what are the implications?
- What new management philosophies or procedures may be instituted as a result of integrating the two organizations? What is the timetable?
- How will attitude issues be handled? Considering the impact of acquisition on the work force of the acquired company, how will productivity and motivation be maintained? Have any employee surveys been conducted to gauge attitudes?
- Are worker redundancies anticipated?
- Is the organization's decision to pursue an expansion strategy likely to result in turnover? Layoffs? How much is anticipated?
- Does the acquired organization have to meet certain regulatory requirements? Are they the same as, similar to, or different from the kinds of regulatory requirements the acquiring organization must meet?
- Are the two organizations' human resource management policies (such as selection, hiring, appraisal, rewards, or career development) compatible? Must they be modified to be compatible?
- What are the training implications of the acquisition for both organizations? For managers? For other employees? How could training help the acquiring organization reach all or any of its strategic goals?
- How does each organization view training and development? What does the acquired organization's training system look like? Is it centralized or decentralized? Does it emphasize formalized training or on-the-job training, or a combination? Is this compatible with the acquiring organization's views?
- Does the acquired organization have a training department? How large a staff? What are their backgrounds? What kind of training facilities or equipment are there? What kind of relationships with outside providers exist?

- Are the training functions in the two organizations redundant?
- How could training smooth the integration of the two firms? What are the training implications of the merger?
- Does either the acquiring or the acquired organization have an employee educational assistance plan (tuition reimbursement)? How can such a plan be used to enhance worker skills? If both organizations have plans, does one offer more than the other?

When the Strategic Emphasis Is on Diversification

- How many separate buy-outs or purchases are planned?
- How well prepared (trained) are top managers in making informed decisions about the future of the acquired organization and its utility to the organization?
- What are the training implications of building a management team that excels in this arena?

Disinvestment Strategy

Strategic focus includes trimming back and refocusing resources. Strategic emphasis options include retrenchment, turnaround, divestiture, or liquidation in pursuit of a disinvestment strategy.

- Why and how has your organization been competitive in the past?

When the Strategic Emphasis Is on Retrenchment

- What steps does the organization plan to take to retrench? Will it use cost reduction? Asset reduction? Revenue generation? Why?
- How will it build on the past strengths that made it competitive?
- What functional strategies will be employed by the various operating units during retrenchment?
- How can costs be contained in the training department?

- What suggestions could the training advocate make for the organization as a whole to cut costs outside of your department?
- Are there any pieces of equipment that are not used, are not used properly, or have not been properly explained? If so, how will this situation change?
- What technologies or processes does the organization plan to use during retrenchment? Are technological changes or advances anticipated? When? How will these be integrated in light of the organization's limited resources?
- What shifts in organizational culture, behavioral norms, and work-related values will be required?
- How will the existing or remaining work force be affected?
- How will attitude issues be handled? Considering the impact of cutbacks on the remaining work force, how will productivity and motivation be maintained? Should any employee surveys be conducted to gauge attitudes?
- Is there a future goal of developing and implementing a turnaround strategy?

When the Strategic Emphasis Is on Turnaround

- How has the contextual picture changed since the organization began its retrenchment? What does the organization's industry look like? Is the industry stable or evolving? Who are the main competitors?
- How has the organization redefined itself and its goals?
- How will resources be reallocated to support turnaround?
- Does the organization plan to use new technologies or processes as part of the turnaround effort?
- Has your leadership changed? What are the implications of these changes?
- What shifts in organizational culture, behavioral norms, work-related values, management philosophies, or procedures will be required to make the turnaround work?
- Are there any new regulatory considerations?
- What changes must occur in jobs and the skill levels of workers to make the turnaround strategy successful?

- Can current workers meet the challenges of turnaround? What training (and other help) do they need?
- Will the organization be recalling furloughed workers?
- What kinds of new hires does the organization want? Should the organization be looking for a different kind of worker than it has in the past?
- What suggestions would the training advocate have for employee orientation of new hires and rehires?

When the Strategic Emphasis Is on Divestiture or Liquidation

- Does the organization have the resources to provide outplacement counseling or new skills training for employees who will be displaced?
- Are there other training programs that could be provided in areas such as stress management?
- Can outplacement and training be provided or underwritten by a public agency or program? How will this be coordinated?
- What should outplacement and other training look like?
- Are there job opportunities within the organization's geographical area? Has a job scan been conducted?
- In divestiture, the core company tries to remain in business. To what strategy will it shift, and what are the human resource management and training implications?

CHAPTER 9

Connecting Training to Strategic Decision Making: Practical Approaches

As Chapter Eight illustrates, trainers must gather quite a bit of information about their organizations before they can credibly advance the notion of integrating training with other strategic considerations. The development and advancement of ideas about how training can support organizational strategy must be preceded by an understanding of the employer's competitive environment and its "macro" or umbrella strategy for competing in the marketplace as well as a firm grasp of the functional or operational strategies of the organization. In short, any attempts to influence the strategic decision-making process cannot be expected to succeed without a strong knowledge base.

This very base is essentially what top business executives are referencing when they say "you've got to know the business your company is in before you can be a strategic player." Trainers have heard this advice from many, many corners. However, they seldom are told the "punch line": knowledge is one thing, but making training a player in an organization's strategic arena is quite another.

Being knowledgeable and clever about training's potential contribution to strategic goals is only a start. Once the training and development advocate understands the dynamics of an organization's strategic management process and has identified the strategic framework employed by an organization, then the

214

process of influencing the decision-making process can begin.

The good news is that quality intelligence gathering reaps its own rewards; it constructs a strong base for any game plan to influence the decision-making process of an organization. Regardless of how smart a player is or the volume or quality of information gathered, however, it is still going to take a lot of effort to get a foot in the strategic door. Common roadblocks that emerge include dismissing training as a "support" function and therefore not a legitimate strategic consideration, characterizing training as "tangential" to operational responsibilities and therefore to be addressed at that level rather than as a strategic consideration, and painting a picture of training as something that occurs naturally (and, it is implied, informally) as a need arises.

These obstacles and objections can be surmounted, but the training advocate must begin to wear two hats to do so. The trick is to be both a trainer and an in-house lobbyist.

Like all good lobbyists who seek to influence the policies of governments and other organizations, the in-house training lobbyist must gather and use information well. As intelligence gathering progresses (see Chapter Eight), the training advocate must begin formulating a plan for influencing the thinking of the organization's policymakers.

Both intelligence gathering and plan development are likely to be tough — and long-term. Any successful lobbying effort is like a three-legged stool. One leg is information, one is persistence, and one is patience. Shorten or remove any one of the legs, and the stool is likely to collapse.

Choosing an Approach

In lobbying, it is always good to keep in mind the old saying that "there is more than one way to skin a cat." An organization's culture and its explicit and implicit power structures will provide clues to the best way to attempt to influence strategic decision making.

In addition, lobbyists must be flexible. There are a number of routes to strategic integration. Even when the training advocate has a full understanding of an organization's strategic goals and culture, sometimes success comes down to advancing the right alternative to the right person at the right time.

After surveying the landscape, the training advocate may see many avenues to the strategic table. The individual trainer can be a guerrilla, staging an underground effort to weave training throughout the fabric of the organization. Or, if the organization is driven by a strong chief executive officer (CEO) whose very interest in an issue can make it a priority, the training advocate can target that leader and launch an effort to influence his or her view of training. Still another option is for the training advocate to engage in institution building—that is, systematically moving to build a training structure that clearly connects to the strategic objectives of the organization. Lastly, the training advocate may co-opt outside influences to build a training infrastructure underpinned by government policies or incentives such as tax credits and targeted training programs.

Of course, some trainers may find themselves in the enviable position of working for an employer that already integrates training. If an organization's culture considers human resource implications of business decisions, then training will be present at the planning table. Ideally, the ascension of training to the upper regions of the organizational planning process results when top decision makers elevate and actively integrate it into the decision-making process, or when training is a vital thread in the institutional infrastructure, so that its omission from strategic management discussions would be unthinkable.

In most U.S. organizations, however, neither of these ideal situations exists. But, research—and many a foreign competitor—have shown that early consideration of how an organization will dispatch its human resources to meet competitive challenges can bring new technology and management systems on line faster. Planning ahead often results in higher productivity, better quality, and ongoing innovation—all essential to staying at the top of the competitive ladder. Therefore, trainers can either take action to move training into the strategic realm or accept the reality of continual service as a fire fighter.

Building Support from the Bottom Up

Organizations that consider the training implications of their competitive strategies in concert with other tactical factors during the strategic planning process are more successful at targeting their resources and maximizing return on investment. Traditionally, however, American businesses have seen training as an expenditure incurred to "fix" a skill gap or to ready new workers. It is, for many organizations, an afterthought that follows the more pressing debates surrounding capital expenditures and marketing plans. However, this perspective can be changed if the training advocate arms her- or himself with snapshots of training's contribution to the organization's bottom line. Such snapshots will help CEOs and other organizational leaders to get a better fix on training's existing role; from that base of support, the training department can begin to build support for an agenda that will move training into the strategic arena.

One approach to building support is to start from the bottom up by mounting a "grass-roots" campaign. The first step is to establish visible and measurable links between training and the organization's business goals. The case for connecting training to the strategic decision-making process must be crafted brick by brick. This can be done by quantifying training's return on investment, its contribution to productivity, or its role in mitigating the costs of integrating new technology and processes.

Such information should be gathered course by course, training intervention by training intervention. Findings should be put into written reports, and those reports should be sent to the organization's top decision makers. This routine should become a regular part of the training advocate's job. This cannot be overemphasized. If the CEO and other organizational leaders have little or no quantifiable information about training's current contributions to the organization, they cannot be expected to embrace the notion that training should be considered concurrently with other strategic issues. Further, those decision makers will never thoroughly understand training's contribution without quality information from the workers closest to the line—the trainers.

What Should Reports Include? Training reports should include a section that spells out how training is or could be used to support the organization's competitive initiatives and strategic goals. To accomplish this task, the training advocate should use his or her knowledge of the organization's strategic plans, competitive environment, work-force profile, and so on (see Chapter Seven and Chapter Eight). This section should conclude with (1) some *low-key* speculation about how the early and regular consideration of training needs throughout the strategic planning process could make the introduction of new technology, processes, and so on more cost-efficient and -effective; and (2) a recommendation that such concurrent consideration be standard operating procedure in the future.

Last but not least, copies of this report should be sent to those operational departments or divisions most affected by the training and, if the organization has one, to the strategic planning staff. This relatively easy action will serve the training advocate well. First, it represents an effort to reach out and educate other organization players about training's role. Inevitably, the interest of some will be raised, and from this group the training advocate can build a network that communicates the value of training throughout the organization. Also, these efforts show the training advocate as accessible and out front, open to an exchange of ideas and eager to explore notions that may, in the long run, have training implications.

Become a Recognizable Face. Creating a paper trail is just one part of the bottom-up approach. The training advocate needs to begin managing the effort to move training into the strategic decision-making process by "walking around." This variation on the advice of Tom Peters (coauthor of *In Search of Excellence*) to all corporate managers is an important part of building grassroots support for training. Of course, the training advocate should continue to play a support role, supplying training in response to the needs of the organization. However, a more proactive posture must be introduced. In addition to responding to the needs of other departments, the training advocate should begin to ask other departments about their objectives and what they see as the potential training implications of moving toward those goals. This creates two-way communication as the training advocate gathers information about the various departments and divisions of the organization and is transformed into an informal advisor and sounding board for key operational personnel.

In addition, the training advocate can serve as a resource for other departments that are traditionally viewed as "support." The training advocate should provide personnel administrators with information that illustrates the role of training in enhancing individual lifetime earnings and achieving career goals. (Such information is available from the American Society for Training and Development, 1630 Duke Street, Box 1443, Alexandria, Va. 22313.) By portraying training as an employee benefit, personnel administrators may find it a useful tool in attracting and retaining quality employees.

Likewise, accounting personnel should be informed of return on investment (ROI) information that trainers may have gathered during training evaluations. Especially important is any information that illustrates (1) how cost-effective it was when an equipment purchase and training were planned simultaneously or (2) the added costs associated with developing and providing training to mitigate unsuccessful attempts to bring new technology or new management processes on line.

Always keep in mind that organizations are a tapestry of explicit and implicit leadership structures, and that all hold opportunity for influence. Therefore, commitment and support from *both* the formal and informal leadership structures inside the organization should be sought. The explicit (formal) organizational leadership of the organization includes executives, managers, supervisors, union leaders, formally appointed employee representatives, and so on — anyone who holds conferred power, title, and authority. Equally important (and surprisingly influential) is the implicit (informal) leadership structure, which includes undesignated floor leaders, worker spokespersons with obvious followings, unofficial nonsupervisory-level group leaders — anyone who is a leader because she or he is regarded as such by peers, has their respect, or projects a sense of reliability, goal orientation, and vision. It is important to open channels of communication with both kinds of these opinion leaders.

The training advocate can even promote *ownership* of training from the bottom of the organization chart upward. Nonsupervisory employees can become valuable allies. As more organizations move toward participative management, line employees are increasingly asked how to make improvements in productivity and quality. If they see training as valuable, theirs can be a powerful voice. By being candid about training's capabilities, sharing information about the possibilities if training is elevated to a strategic consideration, and seeking their views, the training advocate can build a strong base of employee support. In addition, such communication may short-circuit any resistance to training programs that management later requires as a condition of employment.

All employees, but especially managers and supervisors, are environmental scanners, monitoring and interpreting data. Therefore, all employees are in a position to assess the value of training, either through direct experience in applying new learning to their job or by observing the integration of new learning with job tasks. All should be encouraged to be vocal about the role of training in their work programs, and the training advocate's door should be open to hear supportive comments and criticism. It is important to create an atmosphere that is responsive when legitimate suggestions are made to modify current training programs or to make them more relevant to strategic objectives.

It cannot be overemphasized that support must be sought both horizontally and vertically within the operational structure of the organization. The bottom-up approach will not work if trainers allow themselves to be pigeonholed into the training department, responding to demands but forever out of touch with *emerging and future* needs of the organization. While it seems like a big investment in time and energy to execute many of the suggestions outlined in this section, making such an effort will pay off.

The kind of interactions described here open the door to coalition building. An organization's leadership is more likely to respond to proposals that training be connected to the strategic decision-making process if support for such proposals comes from a variety of sources rather than from just the training department.

Leadership and Institutionalizing Training. The easiest route to the strategic decision-making process is to select a job with a company whose chief executive officer has a personal commitment to continual learning in the workplace. Even the best data are unlikely to persuade an intransigent CEO who sees training as an extraneous cost rather than as an investment to change his or her perspective.

In an enlightened environment training will be represented at the highest levels, and its designated representative will have access to *and* influence with the CEO. Channeling information through this representative and supporting strategic considerations with hard data on training and development are the keys.

Leadership from the CEO provides tremendous leverage for integrating training with the strategic goals of the corporation. When the CEO actively seeks to integrate training and strategic decision making, support from other levels of the institutional hierarchy usually follows.

The CEO also has the authority to begin institutionalizing the role of training in the strategic process through appointment of high-level staff who serve as the focal point for training policy decisions and have direct access to the CEO. If a CEO is supportive of training's strategic role but has not designated such a representative, the training advocate should initiate a dialogue about the creation of such a slot by providing the CEO with written information about companies that use this approach. The designation of a vice-president for training or human resource development who has direct access to the CEO and is a working part of the strategic management team is both symbolic and catalytic in that it elevates the training function to the highest levels of the employer's decision-making process and keeps it a key ingredient in the strategic stew.

Moreover, an executive functioning at a high institutional level has leverage throughout the organization. Under such circumstances, a training advocate has the opportunity to operate as an entrepreneur (intrapreneur), selling training's contribution to plant managers and line managers and making the case for its role in expediting change and integrating technology and procedures. Some corporations use this approach to drive training considerations down through the organization and to create an atmosphere that causes training needs to "bubble up." For example, a vice-president for training/HRD may operate at the corporate level and have a cadre of "agents" in each corporate division or plant who serve as training practitioners, advocates, coalition builders, and information conduits. Using this approach, some companies have developed a strong organizational approach to maximizing their human capital investment by treating training as an essential part of the strategic mix.

While the personal commitment of a CEO to linking training to strategic goals may appear on the surface to be the "miracle" ingredient, it is not without its problems. While CEO support can be powerful, it can also be temporary. With the changing of the guard comes the changing of priorities. Training will not endure beyond a leader's tenure unless advocates can translate leadership vision into administrative processes and structures that guarantee a sturdier commitment. Therefore, CEO support should be viewed as an opportunity to institutionalize the integration of training into the corporate strategic management process.

Carrier Corporation, the world's leading manufacturer of heating, ventilation, and air-conditioning equipment, tackled this concern by placing the training manager on the corporate planning council. Because the training manager was a member of that group, her access to and influence on the strategic decision-making process were institutionalized. The manager was aware of all plans for expansion, reduction, and other operational changes well in advance of their initiation. Training department perspectives were and continue to be incorporated into the planning process and are implemented during execution of the organization's one-year and five-year plans addressing new equipment, personnel, and marketing strategies.

Similarly, Motorola has moved to institutionalize its commitment to integrating training into the strategic decision-making process. The process of identifying or updating corporate strategic goals and their associated training requirements is the responsibility of several senior-level committees. The Motorola Training and Education Center Advisory Board, consisting of the company's senior executives and its chairman, meets twice annually to update and chart the corporate strategic plan and to develop a general budget for each of five broad functional areas. The five Motorola Training and Education Center Functional Advisory Councils, representing engineering, manufacturing and materials, marketing, personnel, and sales, then meet to translate the Executive Advisory Board's training guidance into specific plans for each of the respective functional areas; each council also meets quarterly to prioritize training requirements. Based on this guidance, the center designs and develops training programs and courseware for the organization.

Institutionalizing Training Without Leadership. In the absence of expressed CEO support, training considerations can only be part of the strategic decision-making process when they have a strong institutional underpinning. Even in light of CEO leadership in this arena, *sustained* integration hinges on institutionalized support.

Linking training to strategic goals from the bottom up requires a systematic view of training that emphasizes the interconnection of parts of the organization and the relationship of the organization to its environment.

A systems view of an organization emphasizes that any one system will be unfocused without direction from the larger systems it serves. The identification of organizational objectives provides context, meaning, and direction for the entire organization. To be viable, training must contribute to the goals of departments it serves and, through these larger departments, must contribute to organizational objectives.

A systems approach to training necessitates an information-gathering and decision-making process that defines methods not only for performing training but also for "linking" that training to the goals of systems and subsystems in a support role. In short, a training "infrastructure" must be built.

Training can be leveraged inside the institution. Course by course, training must be shown to further the objectives of the organization, and instructional programs must be designed to facilitate the attainment of corporate goals. Training should be buttressed by learning objectives, working team objectives, and strategic objectives. It should be made clear that training moves the company forward in tactical and strategic ways.

In the absence of CEO support, this is a tough road to travel. However, the training advocate can advance the strategic role of training by utilizing some tools that are readily available. By designing and implementing evaluation approaches that clearly illustrate how a training intervention supports the organization's goals and objectives, the training advocate can begin to amass the kind of information that makes strategic planners and operations managers believers and allies. Second, the use of accounting structures that look at the return on investment for training expenditures provides hard data on the cost and cost-effectiveness of training. The use of either or both of these tactics to institutionalize consideration of training can lay the groundwork for movement into the strategic arena.

Using External Resources. Training sometimes is catapulted into the strategic decision-making process because it is a tool for addressing some outside force. Many industries must consider training as part of their overall agenda because federal, state, or local law drives them toward compliance with certain specifications.

For example, many industries must conduct training in areas such as safety, hazardous waste handling, and air and water quality standards; such training is heavily regulated by the Occupational Safety and Health Administration, Environmental Protection Agency, Department of Transportation, and other federal and state agencies. Workers simply must be aware of certain procedures and processes; noncompliance may result in fines or other penalties for the employer.

Because of the importance of such issues and their legal implications, most organizations view them as strategic considerations. The training advocate should work to see that the training department has a direct line of communication with the technical departments that conduct activities regulated by law. Both departments should work together to plan for training needs concurrently with on-line and emerging regulatory requirements.

Opportunity for linking training to the strategic management process also exists when federal or state programs provide support for increased training. Employers may be able to access new markets or create new products by utilizing new state or federal programs that provide funding support to train workers and create jobs.

The training advocate should open channels of communication with professional associations that track programs that underwrite training (for example, the American Society for Training and Development and its local chapters and the National Alliance of Business). It is useful to get to know the organization's Washington representatives and state contacts. The training advocate should also be aware of federal and state programs and their administrators and legislative "angels" as well as how to access them. Importantly, trade magazines, newsletters, and other periodicals as well as attendance at professional association briefings and national meetings can be useful for keeping abreast of new funding opportunities. Any information that may assist the organization in its pursuit of its strategic goals should be shared with strategic decision makers in your organization.

Sometimes a new legislative initiative or government funding program will spur new training investment that helps an organization fulfill its strategic goals.

It would be a mistake to assume that someone in the organization, such as corporate lobbyists in Washington, D.C., or the state capital, already knows these things. No matter how large the organization, its government affairs representatives may be in the dark about training tax credits or programs. Unfortunately, training and education issues have a hard time competing for lobbying time with other pressing tax and regulatory issues; the lobbying staff is stretched by the sheer volume of legislative and regulatory initiatives. However, the training ad-

vocate can turn this to an advantage by providing regular updates to lobbyists based on information garnered from professional sources. This will be appreciated if provided in a collegial
manner. (A word of caution here, however: ventures into this
arena must not appear to be in the nature of "turf building" or
power grabbing. The training advocate must be seen as a resource and an ally to be effective, just as in any other interdepart-
mental coalition-building effort.)

The training advocate can also advance the cause of training by supporting the development of new research and funding incentives for training through the legislative affairs programs
of professional societies and trade associations. When such
organizations ask for letters or phone calls showing grass-roots
support, backed up by company names, the advocate should
try to comply. The training advocate's voice must be heard if
national and state efforts to promote training tax credits and
other innovative tools for underwriting more employer-provided
training are to succeed.

Keep Trying, But . . .

If an organization views training as a costly necessity and
commits resources to it only when forced by circumstance, then
the training advocate has a long lobbying project ahead. From
building credibility to getting the message across that training
should be linked to other strategic management issues, persistence is the key.

Unfortunately, a trainer may also have to face the harsh
reality that her or his organization will not change and that,
if she or he wants to work where human resource and other
strategic decisions are integrated, the only option is to move
on. This advice is not given lightly, nor is it intended to provide an easy out. If trainers follow much of the advice in this
and the preceding chapters and exercise patience and are tena-
cious, then they are likely to make a difference inside organizations.

However, if the leadership is intransigent or myopic, it
may be best for a trainer to take his or her talents to another

environment. What has been learned during this lobbying process, however, can be applied at a new organization.

Above all, trainers should be realists. The more sophisticated trainers become in observing strategic movements, building support groups, and advancing the case for training, the more valuable they become as total executives. Add these talents to training expertise, and the trainer's chances for personal success are multiplied.

PART 4

Policy Recommendations

CHAPTER 10

How Employers, Educators, and Government Can Improve Training

Employers, educators, and governments have frequently assumed an overlapping posture in their responsibility toward human resource development in the United States. Each group has a clear competitive advantage in delivering some aspect of job-related learning, but no institution has an exclusive monopoly on all of its aspects. The lack of demarcated roles is further complicated by geographical diversity — every institution is a major provider of learning somewhere, but no institution covers the entire nation.

Moreover, private and public human resource policies, which previously focused on social policies for the people last in line, now incorporate the growing demand for using human capital development not only to improve the employment security of *all* Americans but also to enhance our nation's competitiveness in the world economy. The time has come to sort through these policies and create a comprehensive strategy that emphasizes both supply-side strategies to improve the quality of learning inside and outside the workplace and demand-side strategies to encourage individuals and employers to invest in human capital.

This chapter proposes a set of training and development policies for employers, educators, and governments — the partners in the learning enterprise. A closer look at these proposals is the subject of *Training America: Strategies for the Nation* (Carnevale and Johnston, 1989), one of the many publications of this government-sponsored project.

231

Employers

Because of their prominent role as training providers for the nation's workers, employers have a huge responsibility to fine-tune, build on, and improve their learning systems. Generally, they currently invest about $30 billion annually, or 1.4 percent of the national payroll, on formal training and development. Many large companies spend 2 percent of payroll. And some employers make a very substantial commitment to training and development by spending 4 percent.

However, although this investment represents a good start, analysis of the available data and case studies of individual employers leads to the conclusion that most employers' current commitments to training and development are insufficient. To prepare for their jobs, only 11 percent of American employees get employer-provided formal training, and only 14 percent receive informal training from their employers. To upgrade their skills, only 10 percent receive employer-provided formal training, and 14 percent receive informal training from their employers (U.S. Census Bureau, 1987).

Policy recommendation: Overall national targets for employer spending should be pegged to the levels of human resource development characteristic of most of the nation's more successful enterprises. The overall national targets should be increased slowly in two phases.

Phase one: The employer community should set an interim target of spending 2 percent of payroll nationwide, or an increase of $14 billion over current expenditures, for training and development. The interim target would increase total commitments to $44 billion and would increase coverage from the current 10 percent of employees to almost 15 percent.

Phase two: Employers should set an ultimate goal of spending 4 percent of payroll nationwide, or an increase of $58 billion over current commitments, for training and development. The final target would increase commitments to $88 billion and would increase coverage from the current 10 percent to almost 30 percent of employees.

Integrate Resources. In addition to increasing resource commitments, employers will need to integrate human resource development into institutional culture and structure in order to accelerate and cushion the impact of change; encourage learning that drives efficiencies, quality improvements, new applications, and innovations; reduce the time it takes to get innovations to the market; encourage flexibility rather than resistance to change; and provide products and services tailored to customers' needs as well as good customer service.

Policy recommendation: Human resource development should be integrated into the employer institution. The following four factors are essential to the success of this effort:

- Leadership: The chief executive officer must make training a priority.
- Institution building: The training and development executive must be a full member of the senior management team.
- Integration: Line managers throughout the institution must be responsible for training and developing their subordinates.
- Accessibility: Training must be available to all employees, not just white-collar workers or technical professionals.

Use the Applied Approach to Learning. The fundamental strength of employer-based training methods is that they are applied. Applied learning works better than learning in traditional classroom formats because it delivers new knowledge in a context meaningful to the learner. New knowledge delivered in the context of work activities motivates learners and can be put into use immediately. Too often, however, employers do not use their natural applied learning methods but rather transfer the deductive methods characteristic of the schools into the workplace.

Policy recommendation: Employers need to use an applied approach to developing workplace curricula. To the extent possible, learning should be embedded in work processes.

Connect Training to HRM Systems. If teaching and learning are to become part of everyday management and supervision, they must be connected to performance-based selection, appraisal, rewards, and career development systems. Managers need to select new employees on the basis of their educational preparation to do the job and their capacity to learn on the job. Each appraisal should conclude with a learning plan for improving individual performance. Learning and new ideas should be rewarded. Finally, managers need to advise employees on strategies for using learning to enhance employment security and career advancement.

Policy recommendation: Workplace learning needs to be closely linked to the performance of individuals, work teams, and strategic change processes. Employers need to:

- Connect learning to performance-based selection, appraisals, and rewards systems in the workplace by:

  - Communicating work requirements to educators and selecting new employees on the basis of their academic performance
  - Including appraisals with a training and development plan to improve performance
  - Rewarding employees for learning and contributing new knowledge that results in cost efficiencies, quality improvements, and new applications and innovations

- Build a stronger link between learning and human resource management and the strategic goals of employer institutions

Decentralize Learning Systems. Employers in the modern workplace will need to decentralize their learning systems to push the human resource development activity as close as possible to the point of production and service delivery. Because technical changes have their greatest impact on production and service delivery employees, these employees have the most to learn. Employers need to be aware of the economic value these employees hold for the company and teach them the skills required for their new and expanding role. By the same token, these employees who are most closely linked with product and service delivery have the most immediate experience with the product and the customer, making them prime experts and the first listening post for new efficiencies, quality improvements, new applications, and innovations. As a result, they have much to teach employers.

Policy recommendation: Employers should create two kinds of learning systems:

- *System one:* a training and development structure that teaches employees the required new skills
- *System two:* a training and development system that allows employers to learn from their employees in order to capture cost efficiencies, quality improvements, new applications, and innovations that employees discover during the production, testing, and use of products and services

Foster Learning Linkages. As production and service delivery become more decentralized, component parts and critical services are supplied by subcontractors, vendors, and part-time or temporary employees. Every employer relies on a complex network of other employers to produce its final manufactured good or service. Every employer also relies on the quality of learning systems in other institutions to ensure quality of its own final product or service. Therefore, employers not only need to strengthen learning systems within their own institutions but also need to build stronger linkages with other employers and external education and training institutions.

Policy recommendation: Employer strategies and government policies need to be developed to link employers closely to their networks of suppliers and external education, training, and R&D institutions. More specifically, employers should:

- Set performance standards linked to learning systems for supplier institutions
- Require that suppliers provide quality training to customers to ensure effective use of supplier equipment, components, or services

- Work with the government to provide resources to conduct R&D on best learning practices that link employers to suppliers and external education and training institutions

   Employers also need to link with external education and training institutions to guarantee a supply of educated entry-level employees and to ensure a supply of high-quality upgrading training for existing employees should employers want to buy rather than to provide training internally. Strong linkages can accelerate the transfer of learning to everyone's advantage.

   Policy recommendation: Employers should communicate new knowledge and changing skill requirements to educators as they accumulate in the workplace.

   Policy recommendation: Employers should embed schooling in the career development process by giving more weight to educational attainment and achievement in hiring decisions.

   Policy recommendation: Employers should work with educators to develop and provide "learning and earning" curricula that combine academic and applied learning experiences.

Educators

   Employers depend on educators to provide job-ready and training-ready entry-level employees. In 1985, 28.1 million workers (about 30 percent of the American work force) reported they had received some or all of their qualifying training from schools. Most (about 16.1 million workers) got their qualifying training from four-year postsecondary institutions. About 5 million got their jobs as a result of training in junior colleges or technical institutes. Another 5 million got some or all of their qualifying training in high school vocational education courses. Roughly 2 million qualified for their jobs as a result of training in private postsecondary vocational schools, and 1.5 million qualified as a result of training in public postsecondary vocational schools (Carey, 1985).

   Employers also buy training from educators to upgrade employee skills and performance on the job. These linkages, described in Chapter Five, create an expanded role for educators in our nation's new workplace. To meet the challenges of preparing and upgrading the competitive work force in today's society, educators need to change some of their basic policies. More specifically, educators must:

- Teach future employees how to make decisions, how to solve problems, how to learn, how to think a job through from start to finish, and how to work with people to get the job done
- Link the teaching of academic subjects to real-world applications
- Work with employers to strengthen the link between learning in school and learning on the job

Whether or not the education system can be reconstructed to incorporate alternative academic and applied learning tracks, it is clear that young people will continue to combine schooling and work. Educators and employers should ensure that work provides some developmental benefits and should carefully integrate the two kinds of learning experiences.

Policy recommendation: Schools, parents, and employers should work together to provide students with opportunities to earn and learn at the same time by participating in work experiences carefully selected and structured to complement academic programs.

Invest in Occupational Preparation. The half of high school graduates who do not go on to postsecondary education require special attention. As discussed in Chapter One, the United States is competitive in the educational preparation of white-collar and technical professionals but is less than competitive at providing basic education and occupational training to non-college-bound youth. Eventually, those youths become the nation's hands-on production and service delivery employees and have substantial control over the efficiency, quality, and development of new applications for products and services. As new technologies and decentralized organizational structures increase skill requirements, those youths will become ever more critical to the nation's competitiveness. Therefore, their educational preparation will increase in importance.

Policy recommendation: The 45 percent of American high school students who are tracked into the watered-down general curriculum and the 19 percent who are in vocational courses should have a new curriculum that mixes solid academic basics and applied learning.

Policy recommendation: The high school vocational system should strengthen the occupational preparation it provides, but not in narrow or dead-end job categories. Instead, students should be given preparation leading to further education or training in postsecondary institutions or by employers.

Policy recommendation: High school vocational education should include a mix of campus learning and carefully structured applied learning in the workplace to accommodate different learning styles and to allow students to learn and earn at the same time.

Open Quality Communications with Employers. To get the most out of the nation's human capital, employers and educators will have to become more closely linked and accountable to one another. If the nation's educators become more accountable to employers, employers will give more weight to educational preparation in making hiring decisions, which will encourage students to take schooling more seriously. Educators can close this current gap by working simultaneously to incorporate employers into their system while bringing students into the employers' framework.

Policy recommendation: The nation's educators need to bring employers into the education structure by involving employers in curriculum development and by providing employers with records that assess academic performance and behavioral attributes of students. Educators need to bring students into the employer structure by focusing learning and performance evaluation on groups as well as on individuals and by deemphasizing pure reasoning in favor of learning experiences that imitate real-world situations and involve physically manipulating objects and tools.

Government

A comprehensive improvement in the quality of learning on the job will have to be driven by both public and private efforts. Clearly, employers and educators will have to make real commitments to making improvements. However, not all of them can afford such commitments unless federal and state governments offer some help.

The United States must expand its original public policy goals in education and training. First, the strategy should include both social and economic policy goals, use human capital development to promote individual opportunity and institutional competitiveness, target both disadvantaged and working Americans, and deliver human capital development both outside and inside the workplace. Second, government policies should encourage better use of scarce resources, including the coordination of existing programs at the point of delivery and closer links among the nation's providers of human capital development. Third, the government should pursue both supply-side strategies that improve the capacity of institutions to provide education and training and demand-side strategies that encourage employers and individuals to invest more resources in education and training.

The current federal system established by the Job Training Partnership Act represents the state of the art in public programming to provide employment and training services for the disadvantaged. It is structured to encourage strong private participation. However, the program demonstrates fundamental flaws. Because funds are limited, and accountability is based on the number of people who find work through the program, administrators often concentrate on those clients who can be moved off the unemployment rolls with minimal effort and cost. There is also a temptation to use JTPA monies for training relatively advantaged employees to prevent dislocation or encourage economic development.

JTPA programs try to rescue four different kinds of clientele: people who have major human capital deficits and cannot get and keep jobs, poor and unemployed people who are quali-

fied for work but are not able to find it, employed workers who
need retraining, and employers who need trained employees to
be competitive. Thus, the program's goals include both institutional competitiveness and individual economic independence.
The current accountability standard, however, tends to serve
the purposes associated with only the second client group — the
poor and unemployed who are qualified but cannot find work.
As JTPA is presently constituted, it violates a cardinal rule of
public policymaking: that every policy goal should be matched
with its own policy instrument and accountability standard.

   Policy recommendation: The basic structure of the JTPA
is sound, and the current programmatic emphases should be
continued:

- Responsibility for programs for the disadvantaged should
  reside with the state and local governments.
- Employers should be assigned a substantial role in the planning and oversight of those programs.
- Programs should emphasize human capital development
  through work and learning rather than income maintenance.
- Performance standards should be a key operational component.
- Programs should provide "one-stop shopping" for clients by
  coordinating human services at the state and local levels.

   Policy recommendation: The JTPA system should move away
from its current "one-size-fits-all" eligibility, treatment, and accountability system. Legislation should separate clients, treatments, and evaluative standards into four groups:

- The majority of resources should be targeted on people who
  are poor and unemployed and demonstrate significant human
  capital deficits. Programs for these people should emphasize
  human development. Accountability should be based on
  measured changes in skills. All services should be fully
  funded by public authorities.
- Poor and unemployed people with marginal human capital
  deficits should be given transitional services, such as job-
  search assistance and subsidies, to move them into the work-

place. Accountability should emphasize transitions into the workplace. Services should be fully funded by public authorities.

- Employed workers who need upgrading to keep their jobs should be given retraining jointly funded by public authorities and employers. Programmatic accountability should focus on increased employability.

- Employers allotted public funds to improve their competitive performance should share costs (provide matching funds) with public authorities. Funding should be available for management development, supervisory training, and technical training (for scientists, engineers, technicians, and craft and skill workers). Funding should not be allowed for executive development or sales training. Accountability should be enforced through matching-fund provisions that stipulate that employers should pay most of the cost of the training.

Provide Human Capital Development to the Disadvantaged. The disadvantaged have the first claim on public attention and public resources. The nation is already past due on its commitment to provide equal opportunity for participation in the American culture, polity, and economy. The litmus test of that commitment is willingness to provide public resources to make every American capable of getting and holding a job, because people unable to get work disappear from the community, drop out of the political system, and fall into the underground economy.

Providing human capital development for the disadvantaged would do more than honor commitments to equal opportunity. It would also pay off in dollars and cents, because investments in young people on the job would help our nation stay economically competitive.

Policy recommendation: In order to provide human capital development at resource levels that can make real improvements in the employability of the disadvantaged, the government should:

- Establish eligibility requirements that distinguish carefully between people with developmental deficiencies and those who require less extensive services

- Establish programs that offer a sequence of treatments from basic human capital development to transitional services, such as job search assistance and hiring and training incentives for employers
- Establish accountability standards for developmental programs that measure progress in skill acquisition and employability
- Establish accountability for transitional services that emphasize job placements and job tenure

Policy recommendation: In order to utilize existing resources more efficiently and provide comprehensive services, services should be delivered in coherent packages tailored to the needs of individual clients. This approach will require common intake and eligibility criteria to provide "one-stop shopping" and programmatic accountability that focuses on the progress of clients rather than on the delivery of a particular service.

Craft Programs for the Dislocated. Experienced employees who become unemployed after several years on the job also have an important claim on federal resources. The same destructive processes are at work for the dislocated as for the disadvantaged. The disadvantaged tend to start out and end up at the bottom of the economic heap. The dislocated experience an economic loss that rarely results in persistent poverty but probably does involve an equal amount of suffering. Dislocated employees are hurt not so much by where they land as by how far they fall.

Dislocation is here to stay. The harsh reality is that a fair trading system and new technology will inevitably benefit all Americans in the long term, but some will be hurt in the immediate future. In the end, practical necessity and compassion suggest the need for policies to address the immediate problems of job dislocation.

Policies for the dislocated need not be expensive. Fewer than one million experienced American employees are dislocated each year. The current proposal for expanding the $30-billion unemployment insurance system beyond its current emphasis on income maintenance is worthy of consideration.

Policy recommendation: The government should incorporate three principles in crafting training programs for the dislocated:

- The nation should set a higher hitch in the safety net for dislocated employees and help them avoid a free fall from middle-class status into poverty.
- Prior notification, counseling, job search assistance, and outplacement should be encouraged while employees are still on the job.
- Dislocated employees should receive counseling and job search assistance first and then training when a job prospect is evident or in hand. If possible, they should receive training on the job.

Target the Employed. Although demographic and economic trends suggest urgency in addressing the education and training needs of the traditional public clientele — the disadvantaged and dislocated — those trends also suggest that the mass of mainstream employees and employers are now appropriate targets of public education and training policy. Trends in the workplace suggest that the need for flexible institutions will reduce the commitment between employer and employee, forcing employees to take more responsibility for their own career development. If they are to do so successfully, they will require new tools, including portable health care, portable pensions, day care, parental leave, and access to job-related training.

Policy recommendation: A government policy to improve access to training for adult Americans should include five components.

- *Part one:* Federal and state governments should experiment with a mix of loans and grants paid for by dedicated taxes and made available to individuals for skill improvements.
- *Part two:* The centerpiece of any strategy to improve the quality of work-related learning must be investment incentives to increase the standing of learning in the American workplace. They should be delivered as tax-based investment incentives providing partial subsidies for the developmental and delivery costs of training.

- *Part three:* Federal and state governments should encourage state and local experimentation and partnerships between employers and state and local authorities to promote better job-related information and more effective transitions from schooling into the workplace.
- *Part four:* Federal and state governments should encourage state and local experimentation and partnerships between employers and state and local authorities to promote:

  - The development of curricula that mix academic and applied learning delivered in both the classroom and work settings
  - Research and development on curriculum and delivery of training in particular occupations
  - The collection, evaluation, and dissemination of best practices in training for specific occupations
  - The development of performance standards for individual occupations

  The institutions receiving these grants should be trade and professional associations, unions, schools, and other institutions that represent members of occupations, provide training in occupations, or represent industries with a concentration of employees from particular occupations.
- *Part five:* To encourage a more efficient use of the nation's learning institutions, the government, in conjunction with employers, should disseminate model practices and provide incentives for employers to off-load the more generic kinds of training into external education and training institutions.

Provide Employers with an Investment Incentive. The absence of a learning infrastructure on the job is the missing link in the partnership between schools and employers. To the extent that learning is embedded in the economy, the economic importance and the leverage of preemployment education and training will increase. To the extent that learning becomes more connected to job performance and economic rewards in the economy, students and trainees will be more interested in their own development. Moreover, to the extent that employers rely on training as a strategic tool, partnerships will be strengthened between employers and the education and training community outside the workplace. Employers will be more interested in well-prepared entry-level employees who are ready to be trained. Employers that upgrade their employees will find more use for external educational and training institutions. Large employers already buy 30 percent of their upgrading training, worth more than $10 billion, from outside suppliers. Smaller employers buy almost all their training from outside resources. The ideal device for expanding employer training — homemade and bought — would be some form of investment incentive for employers to increase their spending on training.

Policy recommendation: Public and private institutions should establish infrastructure to conduct R&D; to inventory, analyze, evaluate, and model best practices in job-related learning; and to disseminate results to employer institutions.

Policy recommendation: The demand-side approach to improving opportunities for job-related training should be accompanied by a supply-side strategy that would increase the institutional capability of suppliers to provide high-quality training to employers and employees.

Policy recommendation: The federal and state governments should encourage state and local experimentation with training programs intended to upgrade employees in the interest of their own career development and in the interest of improving the competitiveness of state and local employers.

References and Suggested Readings

Abell, D., and Hammond, J. *Strategic Market Planning: Problems and Analytical Approaches.* Englewood Cliffs, N.J.: Prentice-Hall, 1979.

Albrecht, K., and Zemke, R. *Service America!* Homewood, Ill.: Dow Jones–Irwin, 1985.

Allen, R. (ed.). "Perspectives on Partnerships." *Career Training, Journal of the National Association of Trade and Technical Schools,* 1985, *2* (1), entire volume.

Betz, F. *Managing Technology: Competing Through New Ventures, Innovation, and Corporate Research.* Englewood Cliffs, N.J.: Prentice-Hall, 1987.

Bishop, J. *On the Job Training in Small Business.* Washington, D.C.: U.S. Small Business Administration, 1982.

Blumenthal, M., and Dray, J. "The Automated Factory: Vision and Reality." *Technology Review,* Jan. 1985, pp. 30–37.

Borquist, B. "The Community College Approach to Serving Business and Industry." *Community Services Catalyst,* 1986, *16* (4), 19–21.

Brown, S. M. *A Primer for Colleges Who Intend to Provide Training in Industry.* Boston: Massachusetts State Commission on Postsecondary Education, 1981. (ED 210 069)

Bureau of National Affairs Staff. "Training to Target Managers." *Bulletin on Training,* 1988, *13* (3), 1.

Cantor, J. A. "A Local Industry Solves Its Training Needs: A Cooperative Training Venture That Works." Paper presented at the national conference on technical education of the

247

American Technical Education Association, Charleston, S.C.,
Mar. 30, 1985. (ED 253 749)

Carey, M. L. *How Workers Get Their Training.* Washington, D.C.:
U.S. Department of Labor, Bureau of Labor Statistics, 1985.

Carnevale, A. P., and Johnston, J. W. *Training America: Strategies
for the Nation.* Alexandria, Va.: American Society for Training and Development, 1989.

Charner, I., and Fraser, B. S. *Different Strokes for Different Folks:
Access and Barriers to Adult Education and Training.* Report no.
ISBN 0-86510-05403. Washington, D.C.: National Institute
for Work and Learning, 1986a.

Charner, I., and Fraser, B. S. "Fast Food Jobs: The Early
Career Training Ground." Book review in *Training and Development Journal,* 1986b, *40* (5), 133-134.

College Board in Cooperation with Policy Studies in Education.
Training by Contracts: College-Employer Profiles. New York: College Board in Cooperation with Policy Studies in Education,
1983.

Cote, E. M. "Miami-Dade Community College: An Organizational Response to Language and Communication Needs of
Business and the Professions." *Proceedings of the Eastern Michi-
gan University Conference on Languages for Business and the Professions,* 1985, *4,* 73-88. (ED 271 978)

Cothran, T. "Build or Buy?" *Training,* May 1987, pp. 83-85.

Cravens, D. *Strategic Marketing.* (2nd ed.) Homewood, Ill.: Irwin,
1987.

Cummings, O. W. "Cooperation Between Business and Education to Meet the Challenge of a Changing Environment." *Journal of Instructional Development,* 1986, *9* (4), 2-6.

El-Khawas, E. "Campuses Weld the Corporate Link." *Educational Record,* 1985a, *66* (2), 37-39.

El-Khawas, E. *Campus Trends, 1984.* Report no. 65. Washington,
D.C.: American Council on Education, Feb. 1985b.

Foster, B. G. "Higher Education and Corporate Education:
From Cold War to Detente to Active Collaboration." *Community Services Catalyst,* 1986, *16* (1), 2-7.

Fraser, B. S. *The Structure of Adult Learning, Education, and Train-*

ing Opportunity in the United States. Washington, D.C.: National Institute for Work and Learning, 1980.

Freeman, R. "The Decline in Economic Rewards to College Education." *Review of Economics and Statistics,* Feb. 1977, pp. 18–29.

Fresina, A. J., and Associates. *Executive Education in Corporate America: A Report on Practices and Trends in Eight Major Industries.* Palatine, Ill.: Executive Knowledgeworks, 1986.

Fresina, A. J., and Associates. *Sales Training in America.* Palatine, Ill.: Executive Knowledgeworks, 1988.

Fullerton, H., Jr. "Labor Force Projections: 1986–2000." *Monthly Labor Review,* 1987, *110* (9), 19–29.

Geber, B. "Supply Side Schooling." *Training,* Apr. 1987, pp. 24–30.

Godfrey, E. P., and Holmstrom, E. I. *Study of Community Colleges and Vocational-Technical Centers, Phase I.* Washington, D.C.: Bureau of Social Science Research, 1970.

Gold, G. G., and Charner, I. *Higher Education Partnerships: Practices, Policies, and Problems.* Report no. ISBN 0-86510-052-7. Washington, D.C.: National Institute for Work and Learning, Apr. 1986.

Gooler, D. D. "Higher Education and Business Relations: The Case of the Education Utility." *Journal of Instructional Development,* 1986, *9* (3), 10–16.

Gruber, K. (ed.). *The Encyclopedia of Associations.* (22nd ed.) Detroit, Mich.: Gale Research, 1988.

Hamburg, S. K. "Manpower Temporary Services: Keeping Ahead of the Competition." In *Training for New Technology: Part III. Cost-Effective Design and Delivery of Training Programs.* New York: Work in America Institute, 1985.

Hamilton, J., and Medoff, J. "Small Business Monkey Business." *Washington Post,* Apr. 24, 1988.

Hampton, W. J. "How Does Japan Inc. Pick Its American Workers?" *Business Week,* Oct. 3, 1988, pp. 84–88.

Honeycutt, E. D., Jr., Harris, C. E., Jr., and Castleberry, S. E. "Sales Training: A Status Report." *Training & Development Journal,* 1987, *41* (5).

Howard, W. R. *Industry-Specific Training Programs: An Overview.* Information Series no. 314. Columbus: National Center for Research in Vocational Education, Ohio State University, 1986.

Huddleston, K. F., and Fenwick, D. "The Productivity Challenge: Business/Education Partnerships." *Training & Development Journal,* Apr. 1983, pp. 96–100.

Johnston, W. *Workforce 2000: Work and Workers for the Twenty-First Century.* Indianapolis, Ind.: Hudson Institute, 1987.

Kargbo, C. S. "Organizational Analysis, Articulation, and Multiple-Option Programming: An Approach to Developing Occupational Curricula." *C.V.A./A.C.F.P. Journal,* 1986, *22* (2), 2–5.

Kimmerling, G. F. "The Youth Market: A Valuable Resource." *Training & Development Journal,* 1986, *40* (7), 78–83.

Kirkpatrick, F. "Training Within Industry: Final Report and Supporting Documents. U.S. Training Within Industry, 1940–1945." In *Inventory of the Records of War.* Washington, D.C.: Manpower Commission, Record Group 211, National Archives and Records Service, 1973.

Kotter, J. P. *The General Manager.* New York: Free Press, 1982.

Lee, C. "Where the Training Dollars Go." *Training,* 1987, *24* (10), 51–65.

Light, G. "Financial Education Programs Are a Super-Growth Industry." *Bottomline,* Sept. 1984, pp. 60–64.

Liston, E. J. "The CCRI [Community College of Rhode Island] Electric Boat Program: A Partnership for Progress in Economic Development." Paper presented at the annual conference of the National Council for Occupational Education, San Diego, Calif., Oct. 1986. (ED 275 373)

Lloyd, J. H. "The Opportunity of Private Sector Training." *Vocational Education Journal,* Apr. 1987, pp. 20–22.

McKenzie, J. "Education: Meeting the Professional Development Needs of Executives in the Mid-Eighties." *Credit,* 1986, *12* (2), 23–26.

Miles, R. E., and Snow, C. C. *Organizational Strategy, Structure, and Process.* New York: McGraw-Hill, 1978.

Miller, V. A. "The History of Training." In R. L. Craig (ed.),

Training and Development Handbook. (3rd ed.) New York: McGraw-Hill, 1987.

Mizrahi, M. "Degrees of Excellence." *A&SM,* Jan./Dec. 1982, pp. 7–10.

Moser, K. "Business-Industry Linkages with Post-Secondary Institutions: Implications for Building Successful Partnerships." *Lifelong Learning,* 1986, *9* (7), 4–5, 27–28.

Moser, K., and Seaman, D. "Implications for Potential Linkages Between Business-Industry and Higher Education." *Adult Education Quarterly,* 1987, *37* (4), 223–229.

National Alliance of Business. "A Year Later, the Compact Sites Take on a New Look." *Work America,* 1988, *5* (5), 46.

National Center for Research in Vocational Education. *Patterns of Linkage Between Training Institutions and Private Sector Employers.* Columbus: National Center for Research in Vocational Education, Ohio State University, Sept. 1982.

National Commission on Excellence in Education. *A Nation at Risk.* Washington, D.C.: U.S. Department of Education, 1983.

National Crime Prevention Council. *A Tale of Three Cities: Security Education Employment Program.* Washington, D.C.: National Crime Prevention Council, 1987.

National University Continuing Education Association. *Challenges for Continuing Higher Education Leadership.* Washington, D.C.: National University Continuing Education Association, 1987.

Newsome, C. "Training Takes on a More Vital Role." *Presstime,* Oct. 1987, pp. 20–27.

Parnell, D. *The Neglected Majority.* Washington, D.C.: Community College Press, 1985.

Pearce, J. A., II, and Robinson, R. B., Jr. *Strategic Management: Strategic Formulation and Implementation.* (2nd ed.) Homewood, Ill.: Irwin, 1985.

Porter, M. E. *Competitive Strategy: Techniques for Analyzing Industries and Competitors.* New York: Free Press, 1980.

Porter, M. E. *Competitive Advantage: Creating and Sustaining Superior Performance.* New York: Free Press, 1985.

Quinn, J. B. "Managing Innovation: Controlled Chaos." *Harvard Business Review,* May/June 1985, pp. 73–84.

Rhinehart, R. L. "Industry-College Cooperation: New Components, Barriers and Strategies." Paper presented at the sixty-second annual convention of the American Association of Community and Junior Colleges, St. Louis, Mo., Apr. 2, 1982. (ED 215 739)

Scharf, J. S. "Thirty-Eight Partnership Strategies: Industry and Technical Institute." *C.V.A./A.C.F.P.*, 1986, *22* (22), 6-9.

Scharlatt, H. "Customized Training: Great Work If You Can Get It." *Training,* Aug. 1983, pp. 42-44.

Schweiger, D. M., Ivancevich, J. M., and Power, F. R. "Executive Actions for Managing Human Resources Before and After Acquisition." *Academy of Management Executives,* 1987, *1* (2), 123-138.

Shoemaker, B. R. "Linkage with Industry." *Vocational Education Journal,* Dec. 1985, pp. 36-37.

Sims, C. "Business-Campus Ventures Grow." *New York Times,* Dec. 14, 1987, pp. D1, D3.

Sonnenfeld, J. A., and Ingols, C. A. "Working Knowledge: Charting a New Course for Training." *Organizational Dynamics,* Autumn 1986, pp. 63-79.

Stephen, E., Mills, G. E., Paw, R. W., and Ralphs, L. "HRD in the Fortune 500." *Training & Development Journal,* 1988, *42* (1), 26-32.

Stern, S., Collins, R. H., and Streit, L. D. "Industry-Education Collaboration: A University Role." *Journal of Industrial Teacher Education,* 1986, *23* (2), 62-68.

Stevens, D. W. "State Industry-Specific Training Programs: 1986." Unpublished paper, Ford Foundation grant, Department of Economics, University of Missouri, Columbia, Dec. 1986.

Strobach, S. K. "Business and Post-Secondary Education Linkages." *Training & Development Journal,* Dec. 1976, pp. 8-11.

Thomas, H. B., Cameron, J. G., and Tuviera, S. P. *Linkage Between Vocationally Trained Participants and Industry Registered Apprenticeship Programs: An Implementation Manual.* Project no. STAR 81-040. Tallahassee: Department of Educational Leadership, Florida State University, Aug. 1983. (ED 273 846)

Tindall, L. "Linkages: Effective Keys to Success." *Wisconsin Vocational Educator,* 1986, *10* (1), 1, 18.

Troyer, D. K. "The Business and Industry Center: A One-Step Storefront Approach." Paper presented to the fall conference of the National Council for Occupational Education, Denver, Colo., Oct. 1985.

Tung, R. L. "Selection and Training of Personnel for Overseas Assignments." In P. D. Grub, F. Ghadar, and D. Khambata (eds.), *The Multinational Enterprise in Transition.* (3rd ed.) Princeton, N.J.: Darwin, 1986.

Unger, R. "Industry Training in a High School." *Vocational Education Journal,* 1986, *61* (7), 33–34.

U.S. Bureau of Labor Statistics. "How Workers Get Their Training." Washington, D.C.: U.S. Government Printing Office, 1985.

U.S. Census Bureau. *Survey of Participation in Adult Education.* Washington, D.C.: U.S. Government Printing Office, 1987.

U.S. Department of Defense. *Military Manpower Training Report FY 1989.* Washington, D.C.: U.S. Department of Defense, 1988.

U.S. Department of Education. *Digest of Educational Statistics.* Washington, D.C.: U.S. Department of Education, 1987.

U.S. Department of Education, Office of Research and Improvement, National Center for Education Statistics. *Digest of Education Statistics, 1988.* Washington, D.C.: U.S. Government Printing Office, 1988.

U.S. Department of Labor. *Apprenticeship: Past and Present.* Washington, D.C.: U.S. Department of Labor, Employment and Training Administration, Bureau of Apprenticeship and Training, 1987.

U.S. Office of Management and Budget. *Budget of the U.S. Government, Fiscal Year 1988.* Washington, D.C.: U.S. Government Printing Office, 1987.

U.S. Small Business Administration. "Job Training in Small and Large Firms." Washington, D.C.: U.S. Government Printing Office, 1988.

Welch, F. "Effects of Cohort Size on Earnings: The Baby Boom Babies' Financial Bust." *Journal of Political Economy,* Oct. 1979.

Wetzel, J. R. *American Youth: A Statistical Snapshot.* Washington, D.C.: William T. Grant Foundation Commission on Work, Family, and Citizenship, June 1987.

Wheelen, T. L., and Unger, J. D. *Strategic Management and Business Policy.* (2nd ed.) Reading, Mass.: Addison-Wesley, 1986.

William T. Grant Foundation Commission on Work, Family, and Citizenship. *The Forgotten Half: Non-College Youth in America.* Washington, D.C.: William T. Grant Foundation, 1988.

Zaragoza, F., and Huber, R. "Cutomized Training with CBO's." *Vocational Education Journal,* Apr. 1987, pp. 32–33.

Zemky, R., and Meyerson, M. *Training Practices: Education and Training Within the American Firm.* Philadelphia: Higher Education Finance Research Institute, University of Pennsylvania, 1985.

Index

Index